Critical Acclaim for Books by Gen and Kelly Tanabe
Authors of *50 Successful Ivy League Application Essays*,
Get into Any College and *The Ultimate Scholarship Book*

"Upbeat, well-organized and engaging, this comprehensive tool is
an exceptional investment for the college-bound."
—*Publishers Weekly*

"Helps college applicants write better essays."
—*The Daily News*

"Invaluable information."
—Leonard Banks, *The Journal Press*

"A present for anxious parents."
—Mary Kaye Ritz, *The Honolulu Advertiser*

"Helpful, well-organized guide, with copies of actual letters and
essays and practical tips. A good resource for all students."
—*KLIATT*

"When you consider the costs of a four-year college or university
education nowadays, think about forking out (the price) for this little
gem written and produced by two who know."
—Don Denevi, *Palo Alto Daily News*

"What's even better than all the top-notch tips is that the book is
written in a cool, conversational way."
—*College Bound Magazine*

"Offers advice on writing a good entrance essay, taking exams and
applying for scholarships, and other information on the college
experience—start to finish."
—*Town & Country Magazine*

"I would like to extend my greatest appreciation to your *Accepted* publication. I recently applied to Cornell University. I read your book from cover to back, wrote an essay about 'Snorkeling in Okinawa' (which most people criticized), and got ACCEPTED to Cornell. Thank you very much for your help, and I'll be sure to refer this book to anyone applying to college."
–Jason Clemmey

"If you're struggling with your essays, the Tanabes offer some encouragement."
–*College Bound Magazine*

"A 'must' for any prospective college student."
–*Midwest Book Review*

"The Tanabes literally wrote the book on the topic."
–*Bull & Bear Financial Report*

"Filled with student-tested strategies."
–Pam Costa, *Santa Clara Vision*

"Actually shows you how to get into college."
–*New Jersey Spectator Leader*

"Upbeat tone and clear, practical advice"
–*Book News*

ACCEPTED!
50 SUCCESSFUL
COLLEGE ADMISSION
ESSAYS

Fourth Edition

- Your essay can get you in or keep you out of the college of your dreams
- Step-by-step instructions on how to craft a successful college admission essay
- Learn from over 50 essays that worked
- Avoid 25 mistakes that doom any essay

Gen and Kelly Tanabe

Harvard graduates and award-winning authors of
50 Successful Ivy League Application Essays,
Get into Any College and *The Ultimate Scholarship Book*

Accepted! 50 Successful College Admission Essays (Fourth Edition)
By Gen S. Tanabe and Kelly Y. Tanabe

Published by SuperCollege, LLC
3286 Oak Court
Belmont, CA 94002
www.supercollege.com

Copyright © 2011 by SuperCollege, LLC
Previous Editions: © 2002, 2005, 2008

Credits: Cover design © 2011 TLC Graphics, www.TLCGraphics.com. Design: Monica Thomas. Edited by Bob Drews. All essays in this book are used by permission of their authors.

Trademarks: All brand names, product names and services used in this book are trademarks, registered trademarks or tradenames of their respective holders. SuperCollege is not associated with any college, university, product or vendor.

Disclaimers: The authors and publisher have used their best efforts in preparing this book. It is intended to provide helpful and informative material on the subject matter. Some narratives and names have been modified for illustrative purposes. SuperCollege and the authors make no representations or warranties with respect to the accuracy or completeness of the contents of the book and specifically disclaim any implied warranties or merchantability or fitness for a particular purpose. There are no warranties which extend beyond the descriptions contained in this paragraph. The accuracy and completeness of the information provided herein and the opinions stated herein are not guaranteed or warranted to produce any particular results. SuperCollege and the authors specifically disclaim any responsibility for any liability, loss or risk, personal or otherwise, which is incurred as a consequence, directly or indirectly, of the use and application of any of the contents of this book.

ISBN 978-1-932662-95-5

Manufactured in the United States of America
10 9 8 7 6 5 4 3 2 1

Cataloging-in-Publication Data
Gen S. Tanabe, Kelly Y. Tanabe
    Accepted! 50 Successful College Admission Essays / by Gen S. Tanabe and Kelly Y. Tanabe. –4th ed.
        p.   cm.
    Includes appendices and index.
    ISBN 978-1-932662-95-5
    1. College Admission   I. Title
    2. Reference   3. Education

CONTENTS AT A GLANCE

TABLE OF CONTENTS

Chapter 6. Roundtable With Admission Officers / 55

Chapter 7. 57 Successful Admission Essays / 71

Chapter 8. Parting Words / 211

Appendix: Web Resources / 215

Index / 216

SPECIAL SECTIONS

Advice Straight From Admission Officers

These successes and failures as described by admission officers are enlightening and even entertaining. They provide insight into the importance colleges place on essays and what you can do to make the most of the opportunity that the essay provides.

Chapter 6: Roundtable With Admission Officers

We sat down with admission officers to find out what they are looking for in the admission essay. Read their frank advice on what students have done right and wrong. Plus, get valuable tips on how to make your essay stand out from the rest.

This book would not have been possible without the selfless contributions of students and admission officers. They gave of their time and shared their knowledge so that future applicants would benefit.

A special thank you to: William T. Conley, dean of undergraduate admission at Case Western Reserve University; Elizabeth Mosier, acting director of admissions at Bryn Mawr College; Peter Osgood, director of admission at Harvey Mudd College; Lloyd Peterson, former senior associate director of admissions at Yale University and former dean of admissions at Vassar College; Gail Sweezey, director of admissions at Gettysburg College; and Michael Thorp, director of admissions at Lawrence University.

We dedicate this book to the people who helped make it possible and to you, our dear reader, who we hope will use these lessons to create your own successful admission essays and get into the college of your dreams.

CHAPTER ONE

THE ALMIGHTY ADMISSION ESSAY

In this chapter you will learn:

- **Why the admission essay is critical to your college acceptance or rejection**

- **Why college admission is an art and not a science**

- **Who we are & what we can teach you about writing a successful college admission essay**

Why The Admission Essay Is Critical

It is your moment. Your application is about to be read by the admission officer at the college you *really* want to attend. Unfortunately, it has been a long week, and she has already reviewed hundreds of applications from other students. Many of these students have similar grades, test scores and activities. So what will set your application apart from the others? What will keep your application out of the dreaded pile of denials?

The answer is your college admission essay.

The essay is your single greatest opportunity to distinguish yourself as an individual by sharing who you are, what you have learned and what motivates you. In this decision-making moment, will your essay make the most of this opportunity, or will it fall flat on its face?

It all depends on you. You are the creator of your essay, and your effort and skill will determine its fate. But while your future is in your hands, you are not alone. We are here to help. This book will help increase your chances of writing an essay that makes a difference and helps you to receive that coveted thick envelope—an acceptance letter from the college of your dreams. In this book you will learn how to:

See why colleges value essays. By understanding why colleges require essays and what they hope to learn about you from them, you'll have the insight you need to write a powerful essay.

Select the right topic for you. The right essay topic allows you to write with passion and insight. With the wrong topic, you may be afflicted with time-consuming writer's block or even worse write a lackluster, emotionless essay.

Write a successful essay that works. Our comprehensive writing chapters guide you through the entire process. We take you through the first word on the page to the last period in the conclusion. These are strategies that you need to know to write a successful essay.

Avoid costly mistakes. Learn from our 25 essay disasters the common mistakes that can kill any essay and how you can avoid them.

College Admission: Art Or Science?

The former senior associate director of admissions at Yale University discusses the art of college admission

It would be great if college admission were a science with a simple formula to determine whether you were accepted or denied. Grades of x plus test scores of y equal guaranteed admission to colleges a, b and c. It would certainly reduce your stress level to know where you stood in the process.

But the reality is that no single score or grade is a complete reflection of who you are. And college admission is more complicated than a simple formula of x + y = z. It is more accurate to think of college admission not as a science but as an art.

Colleges want to know you both as a person and as a student. They want to accept those who will add to the campus both inside and outside of the classroom. While scores and grades can tell colleges about your academic performance, the essay and other parts of the application reveal more about you as an individual.

We asked Lloyd Peterson, former senior associate director of admissions at Yale University, former dean of admissions at Vassar College and current director of education at College Coach, to answer the question: Is college admission an art or a science?

"I think college admission is much more of an art today than it was 20 years ago. There are fewer decisions made today based on matrices or indices. More decisions are made on qualitative factors and on a stronger balance between preparation and potential," he says.

Peterson says admission officers are aware that this system is not good for your blood pressure. He recalls, "Many moons ago it was more methodical and formulaic. Now it's more like a chess match, which drives the public crazy. The public wants a blueprint. They do not want to wallow around in the gray area. But it's that gray area that makes our job an art."

Considering the selectivity of colleges and the fact that American institutions are the highest rated in the world, it appears that this system, while not perfect, works in matching the right students to the right school.

Save time with recycling. By reusing and editing your writing, you can use one essay for multiple applications. We share tested techniques for doing this effectively.

Understand what colleges want to see in your essay—direct from admission officers. Our distinguished panel of admission officers explain in their own words what qualities make or break essays. This is your opportunity to pick the brains of these experts who have determined the fates of thousands of other applicants like you.

Be inspired from the success of other students' essays. We have brought together over 50 successful essays written by a wide variety of students. Get insight into what worked for these students to gain admission to their dream colleges including Harvard, Princeton, Stanford, Yale, Duke, MIT, University of Pennsylvania, UC-Berkeley, USC, Northwestern, Brown, Cornell, Bard, William and Mary, University of Chicago, University of Michigan, Dartmouth, Rice and more.

In short, this book gives you everything you need to take control of your essay and create the best one possible. It is critical that through your essay you (figuratively, of course!) grab the admission officer by the collar and give her a reason to admit you. By reading this book you are taking the first steps toward this goal.

What We Can Teach You About Successful Admission Essays

You may be wondering who we are and what we know about writing successful essays. As the authors of nine books on admission and scholarships including, *Get into Any College, Get Free Cash for College* and *1001 Ways to Pay for College,* we have had the pleasure of meeting thousands of students and admission officers. In writing this book, we conducted extensive research and interviews with both students and admission officers.

But perhaps more important than this research is the fact that we've been in your shoes. When we applied to colleges, we spent countless late nights agonizing over our essays, fighting cases of writer's block and writing and editing draft after draft. Fortunately, through a combination of hard work, helpful editors and a little bit of luck, we were able to write successful essays and were accepted to every college that we applied to including all the Ivy League colleges. You can even read two of our essays in this book.

We wrote this book so that you would not have to endure the same struggles that we did and that the three million other students who apply to college each year face.

The sum total of our experience, research and know-how is contained within these pages. If you follow the writing strategies and learn from the successful essays, you too can write a powerful admission essay that will help you get into the college of your dreams.

CHAPTER TWO

THE INGREDIENTS OF THE ESSAY

In this chapter you will learn:

- Essay questions you are likely to face

- If college essay questions are really trick questions

- Extra precautions for applying online

Why You Should Care About The Essay

The ancient Chinese general Sun Tzu once wrote, "To know your enemy is to defeat your enemy." Good advice. And while the essay is not your enemy—although at times you may feel that it is—the principle is still the same: Understand what you're up against. So before we jump into the strategies used to write a successful essay, let's be sure that you understand exactly what the essay is and why you should care about it.

If you've looked at a college application, you've probably seen the section titled "Personal Statement." This is just a fancy way of saying essay. Most colleges require one "Personal Statement" of about 500 to 1,000 words, and many also ask for one to three additional shorter essays.

Colleges value essays because they allow them to gain insight into who you are beyond the facts and figures of the application form. For you, this is the opportunity to present your most important strengths, especially those that may not be reflected elsewhere in your application. And it can and does happen that students on the academic borderline cross into the college promised land because of the power of their essays!

By understanding the components of the essay and how to approach each of them, you will have the background information needed to tackle them. There is something to be learned from a 2,000-year-old general after all.

Essay Questions You're Likely To Face

Essay questions can address topics as creative as an unusual item you plan to take to college or as mundane as your favorite class, as specific as an influential piece of music or as broad as anything about yourself. Questions for the essay vary by college in their specificity, originality and flexibility. Some even let you write your own questions.

To give you an idea of the variety you may encounter, here is a small sample of recent questions.

- Describe someone who has had an influence on your life.

- Write your own question and then answer it.

- Describe a book or class that has challenged the way you think.

Is This A Trick Question?

The director of admission at Harvey Mudd reveals what's behind his questions

Tell us something about yourself. This five-word question is one of the most common on college applications. It sounds harmless enough, but for many students it's enough to cause some serious stress. The applicants reason that the colleges wouldn't ask such a simple, straightforward question. It must be a trick. And even worse, they have no idea how to answer it.

We asked Peter Osgood, the director of admission at Harvey Mudd College and former associate dean of admission at Pomona College, why he asks this question on applications. We also wanted the truth about whether there was a hidden meaning to these types of general questions.

"We ask for two essays and give students a choice of several questions. The most obvious question is a simple tell us about yourself. It's not a trick question—we really want to know something about you," explains Osgood.

However, not any old answer will do. As Osgood cautions future applicants, "We don't want to know something that we can get from your application. It's too easy and too safe for a student to write an essay that is purely descriptive about what they have done and accomplished. All of that will be evident elsewhere in the application."

But what happens if students write essays about their achievements without spending the time to go beyond what can be found in their resumes? According to Osgood, this would be a disaster.

"That kind of essay won't shake us up. It's not going to tell us anything new. That kind of essay doesn't help students at all. It's a lost opportunity," warns Osgood.

When you read a question, don't get stuck on finding a deeper meaning or trying to second-guess the intentions of the college. Most questions are what they appear to be—just questions. Instead of searching for a hidden message, focus on how you will answer the question, adding something new to how you present yourself to the colleges.

- What things do you think the admission office should look at when deciding whom to accept?

- What does "good character" mean to you?

- If you could develop a specific skill what would it be? Why?

- Is there anything unusual you plan to bring to college?

- Is there anything that you would like to tell us that is not in the application?

- If you could hold any government position what would it be and why?

- Write about something that is important to you.

- Include a small picture and describe the significance of the photo to you.

Our favorite question, however, comes from the University of Chicago, which is famous (or infamous depending on how you feel) for coming up with extremely creative essay questions. In one recent year the question asked applicants to create their own TV show called "Chicago Survivor" based on the reality TV show. The contestants, the university suggested, could come from any era of human history.

While most colleges are not as creative (or diabolical) as this, they often give you a choice of questions. Some students stress about picking which one to answer. However, there really is no right question. The truth is that colleges don't care which question you answer. Remember that more important than your actual answer to the question is what your answer says about you. Our advice when you are faced with a choice is to pick the question that you can answer most thoughtfully.

The Dreaded Word Count

The college admission essay is one place where brevity is valued. Besides writing the actual essay, most students find that adhering to the word count is the other major obstacle. Often 500 to 1,000 words are all that you are allowed to express the meaning of your life. Some questions will require you to be even more concise—maybe only 300 words. These limits are a challenge to even the best writers, and you must be disciplined in your use of words and sentences. As you are selecting topics, keep the word count in mind—you don't want to choose a topic that would take five pages to thoroughly cover.

On the other hand, having such a strict word count frees you to focus on only the most important aspects of your life and to craft an essay where every word matters. As you write, be aware of the word count. Having a few words over the limit will not hurt you, but if you exceed it by a significant number, say 100 words, then you are going to have to go back to the editing table and figure out what to cut.

Technology To The Rescue Or Not

If you apply by mail you will print essays from your computer and attach them to your application. Some applications leave room for you to write your essay—this is really an artifact from the days when essays were handwritten. Make it easy on yourself and just print your essays on separate sheets of paper.

When printing your essay, be sure to include the question you are answering at the top since many colleges give you choices. Be sure to number your pages so that they are read in the proper order. Also, put your name at the top so if the pages get separated from your application they can find their way back to the right folder.

The Internet has become an integral part of the college application process. You will submit your essays along with the rest of your application online. While this might seem like a convenience, be very careful that you still treat your essay as if it were printed.

We highly recommend that you print your essays to edit them even if you are going to ultimately submit them online. Many college admission officers have told us that while online applications save students time, they have resulted in an increase in the number of careless errors. If you plan on submitting your essays online, be sure that convenience does not inadvertently lead to carelessness.

Now that you know what you are facing, let's look at how to write a successful essay.

CHAPTER THREE

HOW TO FIND THE PERFECT TOPIC

In this chapter you will learn:

- **How to brainstorm a great topic**

- **Questions to jump start your brainstorming**

- **The critical test for originality**

- **Seven questions you must ask before choosing a topic**

- **Dumb topics to avoid**

Begin With A Brainstorm

We recently got an Australian cattle dog named Sushi. To our dismay the first thing she learned was how to successfully coerce humans into giving her people food. Her method was not elegant but very effective. Sushi simply tried every trick she knew—sit, jump, lick, crouch, whine, stare, bark—until she found the right combination. Instinctively she knew that the process of trial and error works.

When it comes to finding the perfect topic, we can all learn something from Sushi. While it is not elegant and relies on much trial and error, the best way to discover a great topic is brainstorming.

To get off to a blustery start, first read all the questions in the colleges' application forms. You want to have these questions in the back of your mind as you brainstorm possible topics.

The key to successful brainstorming is to record every idea that pops into your head. Remember: no topic is too silly, complex or stupid (at least not yet) to write down. To help you get started, ask yourself:

- What are your favorite activities and hobbies? Why do you enjoy them?

- What are your talents or skills? Why did you learn them? Who taught you?

- Who have been the most influential people in your life? The most memorable? The most interesting? Who have you disliked the most?

- What was your best day? Worst? Funniest?

- How have you changed in the past four years?

- What was the most memorable experience you had with your parents? Brother or sister? Best friend? Teacher?

- What accomplishment are you proudest of?

- What makes you special or unique?

- What is your strongest quality?

- What is something about you that is surprising or that other people wouldn't expect?

- What is an interesting conversation that you've had?

- What is a strong belief or philosophy that you hold?

- What annoys you most about other people?

- What have you done during the past four summers? Which summer was the most memorable?

- What is the most difficult or challenging thing you have done?

- When and how have you shown leadership?

- What is the most pressing issue that our society faces?

- What have you and your friends recently talked about?

As you write down ideas, don't rule anything out. Your goal is to give yourself a large number of topics to explore. You should also bring in your friends, teachers and parents for help. Often, great topics are discovered through talking it over with others.

Ideally, you want to brainstorm over the course of a few days. You will need to take breaks. But always keep a pen and paper handy since a good idea can spring up at any moment.

One student we spoke with recalled how he had a brilliant idea while taking a shower. Since he didn't have anything to write with and was so afraid of forgetting the idea, he actually etched a few notes to himself in the steam on the glass shower doors. Other places where students have thought of topics that went on to become successful essays have included: an airplane bathroom, waking up from a nightmare, during a volleyball match and at the zoo.

It's important that you remember that when brainstorming, not all of your ideas will be golden. In fact, some that seemed brilliant when you first thought of them will turn out to be terrible in retrospect. The student who was so excited about his idea in the shower later realized that it wasn't that great once he was clothed and dry.

The Litmus Test For Originality

Once you have a list of ideas, you will need to narrow your choices. For each idea spend a few minutes thinking about what your essay might look like.

A key to writing a successful essay is that it must be original. Therefore, you need to eliminate any topics that would not yield an original essay. One of the best tests is employed by an admission officer who calls it the "Rule of Thumb." Basically, if he can cover the name of the author with his thumb and insert the name of any other applicant, then the essay is not original.

You can perform a similar test on your topics. Think about each topic and what you would write about. Now ask yourself if someone other than you could write this essay. If they could, then the odds are that it will not be original.

For example, let's say that part of your list of possible essay topics includes the following two ideas:

My trip to France taught me that people everywhere are the same.
My Dad has been the biggest influence on my life.

Start with your first idea. In thinking about what you would write about, you decide that the best essay you could produce about your trip to France would be how you realized that while people speak different languages and have different customs we are all basically the same. As an example you might describe how you got to know your French host family and learned that they are concerned with the same issues as your American family.

Now ask yourself: Are you the only one who could write this essay? Do you think many other students have traveled to other countries and discovered the same thing? Is your experience with your host family unique to you? When you think about it, you will likely realize that there is a high probability that many students will write about travel or living abroad and that they too will focus on how they have learned that people from different countries are generally the same. This topic, at least in the way we have described it, is probably not going to be a very original essay. Both the topic is common and what you would write about (your approach) is common.

Next topic. Without a doubt, you already know that dads and moms are going to be common topics. After all, who is not influenced by their parents? So already you see that the topic may not be original. But does this mean you should eliminate the idea?

Not so fast. As you think about how your father has been an influence, you consider how every morning he wakes up to make you breakfast. You also realize that of his many breakfasts, his one specialty is banana pancakes and that he takes great pleasure in preparing this for you. You then think about what this act has taught you about dedication, commitment and not settling for anything but being the best.

Now ask yourself if another student could write this essay. How many will focus on their dads' preparation of breakfast? How many will construct an essay around what they have learned from their dad through his perfection of banana pancakes? Even though dads are written about often, this approach is highly original. This topic may lead to a great essay after all.

Most students find that to be original they will have to find a unique approach to what is often an ordinary topic. You don't need to wrack your brain for an original topic. In many cases, you can be original in your approach to an ordinary topic.

Analyze Your Topic's Revealing Qualities

Besides having an original essay, you need to make sure that it reveals something about you. It cannot just be a mere description of a person, place or thing. You want to reflect on an aspect of your life, preferably one that you are proud of. As you go through your list of topics, eliminate those that are not really important in your life.

Let's examine this by looking at a common question that colleges ask—"What's your favorite book?" The truth is that it doesn't matter if you write about Dostoevsky's *Crime and Punishment* or Doctor Seuss' *Green Eggs and Ham.* What the admission officer really wants to know is what your choice of book reveals about you. It would be a huge mistake to write a book report or analysis of the characters. It would also be a mistake to write about a book that you think is impressive sounding but didn't really have an influence on your life.

Revealing something about you is also more than a simple retelling of your life and achievements. Admission officers expect you to demonstrate your ability to think and analyze through your writing. Therefore, if you simply retell an interesting story of a childhood experience or recount various accomplishments, you will fail to impress them. To uncover something meaningful, you need to spend time thinking and analyzing.

Ask yourself: What did I learn from the experience? Has it changed the way I think? Has it motivated me to act? Make sure you have a topic that will allow you to apply some rigorous analysis. If the topic is shallow or doesn't allow you to present some aspect of yourself then don't write about it.

At this point it may be hard to tell if your topic will make a great essay. However, you should be able to eliminate those that are obviously unoriginal and that won't provide any self-reflection.

Challenge Your Topic With These Questions

Once your topics pass the two tests above, you will want to subject them to a final battery of questions. These questions will help you prioritize those topics with the most potential.

Does your idea have good supporting examples or stories? To be memorable, your essay will need to have concrete details or even anecdotes. You don't want an essay filled with generalizations (again remember that anyone can make a generalization) so you will want to make sure that you have specific detail. Think about details according to your senses—sight, hearing, taste, smell and touch. You want to help your readers develop a mental picture of your experience with your description.

Can your idea be expressed within the limits of the essay? Some topics just require more words to express than you are allowed for your admission essay. While you may not be certain at this stage, you need to be ready to chuck a topic that is just too complex to properly express in approximately 500 words—which is the word limit for most application essays.

Too Much Detail

The director of admissions at Gettysburg College explains why it is possible to reveal too much

The essay can bring out the best and worst in all of us. When we sat down to write our essays it was the first time that we really had a chance to reflect on who we were and what we had done with our lives. While this type of deep thinking should lead to an essay that surprises even you, for some students it becomes an opportunity for confession, for an outpouring of fears, disappointments and anger.

Gail Sweezey, director of admissions at Gettysburg College, has seen more than her share of such essays. According to Sweezey, "Sometimes students can get way too personal in their essays. We want to hear what students have to say, and sometimes students have things happening in their lives that are difficult such as an illness or parents' divorce. It's totally fine to talk about these kinds of things. However, what doesn't work well are essays that go into way more detail than necessary."

As you are writing, be sensitive about topics that are close to you. Remember to take a step back to gain some perspective. Sometimes too much detail can obscure the overall message of your essay.

Will your essay be interesting? This is a very subjective question, but you should try to answer this as objectively as possible. Put yourself in the place of the admission officer who has already read 200 or more essays and has just grabbed yours, which also happens to be the last before he or she can go home. Will your essay pique the interest of this tired admission officer? Will the topic or your approach to the question make the admission officer want to read past the introduction? Just because a topic is original does not always guarantee that it will be interesting.

Can you present the topic in a way that will appeal to a wide audience? Do you need specific knowledge of the topic in order to understand it? For example, the best topic may not be polymerized nanocomposites. Remember who your readers might be. Don't assume that an admission officer has any particular knowledge. They are generally well-read but may not necessarily be able to appreciate a topic that requires in-depth scientific or technical knowledge.

Is the topic truly meaningful to you? Essays about something that you care about are much easier to write and much more interesting to read. Think about all of the writing that you have done in the past. It is much easier and more enjoyable to write about something that you care about than an assignment that you are forced to complete. Help yourself write a better essay by picking a topic that really matters to you.

Can the essay be recycled? Since you will have to write many essays, one of the ways you can reduce this work is to write essays that you can use for more than one college. Often, just by making small changes you can use a well-written essay to answer a similar question by another college. There is more on recycling in Chapter 5.

As you eliminate topics, you will notice that a few will rise to the top as being the most promising. In the next chapter we will put pen to paper or fingers to keyboard. However, before you zoom off to write your masterpiece, we want to leave you with a few words on what we consider to be topics that you should avoid or at least approach with extreme caution.

Just Plain Dumb Topics

There are topics you should avoid. Many of these are obvious, but sometimes students get carried away and write about them anyway. The only exception is if you can "undumb" them by writing about them in an intelligent or unique way. But unless you can do this well (and have your work checked by editors), it is much safer to stay away from these subjects. The taboo topics include:

Sex. While sex sells in advertising, it does not work for college admission. It is okay to write about your experience as a sexual abuse counselor or your volunteer work to prevent premarital sex as long as your focus is on the work that you do and not the explicit experiences of your clients. Remember, this is an admission essay, not a television talk show.

Crimes and misdemeanors. On your application, you are required to report any serious criminal activity, suspensions or disciplinary problems. However, some students feel that even if they were never caught that their candor would be appreciated by the admission officer. Unfortunately, this usually sets off warning signals. As an admission officer, how would you feel if a student spent his entire 500-word essay detailing the number of freeway overpasses that he has marked with his graffiti art?

Of course, petty crimes that were committed when we were children are generally exempt. A great essay could be written about how at age 8 you learned a very serious lesson when you tried to take money out of your mother's purse. It's a very different story, however, when you write about nabbing a purse at age 17.

Drunkenness or getting high. One student thought it would be particularly entertaining to describe how he thought he was a chicken during his last substance-induced high. It may have been entertaining, but it did not gain him admission. No matter how humorous or memorable your alcohol- or drug-induced antics may be, they are not appropriate for your essay. Like tales of criminal acts, they may make the admission officers think you need professional help before higher education.

Drug and alcohol abuse are serious problems on campus—particularly among first-year students. Almost every college has had serious or fatal incidents with underage drinking. This is not something that anyone finds amusing.

Bad grades. Some schools allow a space to offer explanations for poor performance. If there was something that severely affected your grades then you should use this space. However, do not waste your essay trying to justify or make excuses for your poor grades. This is a bad idea since it not only emphasizes that your grades have not been stellar, but it also makes you sound as if you do not take responsibility for your actions or that you tend to look for excuses when bad things happen.

Instead of trying to explain away bad grades, focus on what kept you busy or what kept you motivated. Such an essay will help to convince the admission committee to overlook your lack of academic performance in favor of your other talents and virtues. Admission officers know that not everyone can get straight A's. If grades are not your strong point, show them what is.

Simple description of why the university is perfect for you. The admission officers are already familiar with the beautiful architecture, rigorous academic courses and opportunities to meet extraordinary people at their universities. So you would only be wasting valuable space by simply describing qualities of the college, especially since they probably know more about the college than you do. An exception is if you have a creative way of approaching this. This means that you do more than regurgitate the information from their website or pile on buckets of meaningless platitudes.

A major news story or disaster. There are some events that you can't escape. These stories are in the papers and on the evening news programs for weeks if not months. While these events are extremely important because they have affected a large number of people, they will also be the topic of many students' essays. Because so much has been discussed in the media, for most students there is nothing new to be said. Unless you have a personal connection to the event or a fresh perspective, don't be one of the masses of students to write about it.

Mental imbalances or insecurities. The last thing that admission officers want to read is your self-evaluation of the mental imbalances or insecurities that you have. Surprisingly, some students use the essay as their forum for revealing their deepest insecurities. Some even rationalize that being honest about their shortcomings is the best way to write a genuine essay. You don't need to present yourself as infallible in college admission essays, but you should strive to present yourself in a positive light.

Your plan to create world peace. It is true that admission officers like young people with bright ideas and determination. But when you write a whole essay about your plan to bring about world peace, stop hunger or end poverty, you sound more like a competitor in the Miss America Pageant than an intelligent high school student with a firm grasp of reality. There is nothing wrong with having ideals and dreams, just do not spend a whole essay writing about them. An essay about your dreams of doing the impossible, unless you can back it up with concrete examples of what you have done, will only make you sound unrealistic and naive.

Furthermore, such essays give nothing substantial to the admission officers. Anybody can say they want to end world hunger. More than a few applicants will fall into this trap and write at great lengths what they want to do in the future when in fact they should be writing about what they have already done. Resist any temptation to impress the admission officers with your grand plans since you will end up sounding more deserving of a rhinestone-studded tiara than a mortarboard.

The Big Game. Thousands will write about the Big Game, the Big Match or the Big Tournament. Be careful with this kind of topic since it is so common. If you write about a Big Game, be sure that you have an approach that will be different from the rest. A play-by-play narration of the Big Game is not original. Ask yourself when writing if others have had the same experience and might also write about it in a similar way.

Deep Confessions. If you would be ashamed to read your essay to your parents or friends then it is probably not a good essay to send to admission officers. The essay is your time to shine, not confess something extremely personal. Admission officers want to know why they should admit you to their school, not why you would make a great feature in the gossip column.

Now that you know which topics to avoid, it is time to pick a few ideas from your list and start to write.

CHAPTER FOUR

THE ESSAY-WRITING WORKSHOP

In this chapter you will learn:

- **Essential strategies for writing a great essay**

- **Why you must be the subject of your essay**

- **When the big game is a big mistake**

- **The 25 worst essay mistakes you must avoid**

- **How humor can kill your essay**

Writing Your Masterpiece

Using the finest chocolate in the world does not guarantee a successful souffle. This is because up until the time you serve it, the souffle can catastrophically collapse upon itself. The same is true for your essay. You can start with what seems like the best topic on your list, but once you start writing you may discover that your essay simply collapses.

The only way to see if you can bake—er, make—a successful essay is to actually write it. You will find that some ideas that seemed promising do not translate well onto paper while others that were lower on your list end up making great essays.

Before you start writing, we would like to share with you some important strategies. While there is no limit to the number of ways to write a successful essay, all share common characteristics.

We also want to introduce you to the 25 Worst Essay Mistakes. While these mistakes can doom any essay, they continually appear on essays year after year. Creating a masterpiece means side-stepping these dangerous pitfalls.

Essential Strategies For Writing A Great Essay

It would be great if there were a formula for writing a successful college admission essay—20 percent startling personal realization, 30 percent introspection and 50 percent creativity. Unfortunately, there is no such formula. But there are qualities common to all winning essays. After writing our own essays and from speaking with hundreds of admission officers and successful applicants, here are the characteristics of a winning essay:

Be yourself. It is important to show the admission officers the real you—not who you think they want to see. Explain why you think or act the way you do, what drives you or what has moved you. Speak in your own voice and use your own words. Don't be afraid to write how you really feel. If you have always been jealous of your supermodel pretty sister, say so. It is your true and pure feelings that will make your admission essay stand out.

You Are The Subject Of Your Essay

The acting director of admissions at Bryn Mawr College reveals why you must be the subject of your essay

Throughout this book we have stressed the importance of revealing something about yourself in your essays. Yet if this is a key strategy, why do so many students fail to do this? One reason is because often the question posed by the college asks you to write about someone or something else. How can you write about you when you are being asked to describe someone else?

According to Elizabeth Mosier, acting director of admissions at Bryn Mawr College, students need to realize that regardless of the question, they must write about themselves.

"Let's say that the question asks you to write about an influential person. You should remember that we care less about the person than their influence on you. Use the question as a starting point to tell us about you," says Mosier.

So what should you write about if not about the influential person? According to Mosier, "If you are answering a question about an influential person, focus on why you look at this person as someone significant. Whenever you're answering these kinds of questions, whether it's a story or character portrait, try to give us a glimpse of who you are, your voice and quality of thinking. After all, we are trying to assess what you'll be like as a student on our campus."

When you get a question that seems to ask you to write about something or someone else, be sure to include as much about you as the subject you are outwardly writing about. Remember that colleges ultimately want to learn about you.

Be original. Remember that admission officers have a stack of applications and essays on their desk. How can you make your essay separate from the crowd? By taking a fresh approach to a topic. If you are writing about how your mother is your role model, you could write about how she shows that she loves you by taking care of you, but that would be the common, uninspired approach. Why not take a unique approach? Maybe the best conversations you have with her are while you watch the *Tonight Show* together. Or maybe you have learned patience from the way that she maneuvers through rush-hour traffic. Write in a way that no other student can by writing personally and going beyond surface observations.

Reveal something about yourself. The question may ask about your favorite book, music or class, but the real question is: What do these things mean to you? How have they affected the way that you think or act? Whatever you write about, it should always circle back to you. After reading your essay, the admission officers should have greater insight into who you are, what inspires you and what you aspire to be.

Have a point. Have you ever spoken on the telephone with a friend for an hour and at the end wondered what the conversation was about? That is not the way to impress admission officers. To test if your essay has a clear point, try to capsulize in one sentence what you are trying to convey. If after reading your essay you (or your editors) cannot summarize the central message of your essay in a single sentence, then you need to re-examine it.

Spend as much time thinking as writing. When you are writing—especially under a deadline—it is sometimes convenient to settle for the easiest answer. For example, let's say that you are writing about your decision to become a doctor. You ask yourself, "Why do I want to become a doctor?" You think about it and realize that you always seemed to enjoy helping people. Is that enough? No, go further. Why do you enjoy helping people? Now the answers get harder. Is it because of some early experience when you were a child? Was it because of the influence of your father? Maybe after thinking about it you realize that this is not even the answer at all.

The hardest part about writing your admission essay may not be the writing. To create a successful essay you need to think carefully about what you are going to write and be willing to spend time examining your answers. The best essays begin as simple answers to the colleges' questions. As writers continually ask that nagging question, "but why?" until they can go no further, they transform their essay into a work that contains their best thoughts and ends in a place they hadn't imagined when they started.

As you write, don't settle for easy answers. You may have to take long breaks to reflect. Answers may not come easily, but if you think as much as you write you will be rewarded with an essay that is extremely meaningful and powerful.

Highlight growth. One of the qualities admission officers look for in essays is maturity. They want to know that you are ready to make the transition from high school to college. Use your essay to demonstrate how you've grown or developed over the years. If you are describing a challenge, you might focus on how you overcame it or succeeded despite the obstacle. If you are writing about a failure, concentrate on what you have learned or how you have changed. Colleges want to see that you are introspective about your life, that you can view it with thoughtful perspective. It is very compelling to see in an essay how you have grown as the result of specific experiences.

Keep your introductions brief. You probably know from English class that having a strong introduction is important. However, unlike an essay that you write for class you have a very limited amount of space for the admission essay. Therefore, resist the temptation to overwrite the introduction. Ideally, your introduction should be no more than a short paragraph. Even for a narrative introduction that tells a story or is filled with detail, be careful not to spend too much space on it. Admission officers are primarily concerned with the main points of your essay, not that you have a lengthy, creative introduction. Good introductions are important, but a good introduction alone (without an even better body) has never gotten a student into college.

Create mystery at the forefront. Start the essay with a brief introduction that surprises the readers and makes them want to read past the first sentence. For example, you could start the essay with a description of your fear of the sounds of heavy artillery when you are talking not about your latest trek to the firing range but actually about a phobia of visiting the dentist. Keep in mind that you have limited space and therefore the introduction will have to be fairly brief. Get to the point quickly. And by all means do not get carried away with your own creativity.

Demand 100% from every sentence. Here is a simple test. As you read your work, ask yourself if each sentence makes you want to read the next one. You can take this even further by being as strict with every word. Is each word used purposefully and correctly? Do not just rely on your opinion. Seek the opinions of others. If your essay does not compel the reader to finish, it needs work.

Raise intriguing questions or dilemmas. Ponder questions to which you think the admission officers would be interested in finding the answers. If you raise a question or a dilemma you've faced, ask yourself if the reader would be interested in knowing the results of your decision.

Force yourself to analyze your motivations. When you are writing about your motivations, probe deep into yourself for the answer. For example, if you say that watching a specific concert as a child inspired you to become a musician, identify exactly what it was about the concert that motivated you. Was it the performer's command of the audience? Was it the emotion that the music raised in you? If you are showing cause and effect, carefully and fully explain the cause.

Use original language. Try to describe people, places and events in a unique—but not awkward—style. Think of language as a toy, and play with it. Experiment with dialogue, vary the length of sentences and pose questions. If you use unfamiliar words, make sure you use them correctly. It is better to use ordinary language correctly than to use roller coaster-exciting language incorrectly.

Be witty, but only if you can. Showing your sense of humor will help make your admission essay memorable. If you can make the admission officers laugh or giggle, it will be a definite plus for your application. But do not go overboard with the humor and remember to have someone else check to make sure that what you think is funny really is funny. Your sense of humor may not be shared by your reader. Our advice is to never force trying to be funny. Often you will find that if your story is well told and interesting, inherent humor will show through on its own strength.

25 Worst Essay-Writing Mistakes

In writing a successful admission essay we have found that it is just as important to know what not to do. This list of the worst essay-writing boo-boos comes from years of experience as well as from interviews with admission officers and students. While some seem obvious, it is always surprising how often these mistakes are committed each and every year.

Read this list and then read it again as you are writing your essay.

When The Big Game Is A Big Mistake
Warnings about essays on the big game from the director of admissions of Lawrence University

There are just some types of essays that make admission officers groan. Sometimes these essays are so unoriginal that the admission officers can almost predict their contents. Or, they are so common that literally dozens of students write about the same thing.

For Michael Thorp, director of admissions at Lawrence University, the essay he dislikes is usually about "The Big Game," or a memorable athletic victory.

"It always makes me nervous when young men write about the big game. The big game essays are almost always how they stuck it out and won in the end. I understand that football or any other sport can be very important. But I don't want to read another essay about how their team was down in the last quarter and they gritted their teeth and won," he confides.

He adds, "The message from these kinds of essays is: I'm a tough guy, I gritted it out and that's why I should be admitted. That does not tell me much about the person at all."

There is nothing wrong with writing about sports. In fact, Thorp would love to read an essay about football. But, he says he would prefer to read "how the sport altered your personality or some insight into the metaphysical life on the gridiron. Please, write about sports but just don't send in another essay about how you won the big game!"

1. DON'T try to be someone else. This means you should avoid portraying yourself as Mother Teresa when the closest you have ventured to philanthropy was watching 10 minutes of the Muscular Dystrophy telethon. Often applicants are tempted to create an alter-ego of what they think is the perfect student. Because the essay is a creative effort, it is very easy to stretch the truth and exaggerate feelings and opinions.

How can admission officers tell a fake or forced essay? Easy. Phony essays don't match the rest of the application or teacher recommendations. They may also lack details that can only come from real experiences.

Admission officers have read thousands of essays, and if they believe your essay to be less than the truth, you will diminish your chances of getting in. Besides, we guarantee that there is something about you that has the makings of a stellar essay. If you spend the time developing this in your essay, you will be able to blow the admission officers off their feet in a way that no pretense or exaggeration could.

2. DON'T get stuck on the introduction. In most cases students don't spend enough time on their introductions. Often this is not an irreversible mistake since admission officers are reading for overall meaning. However, for a few students the introduction is where they spend *all* their time. We have seen introductions that took up an entire page. While the introduction was vivid and full of detail, it did not leave enough room for the rest of the essay. Do spend time on your introduction, but don't let it become the best part of your essay. Get the attention of the reader, then move on to the heart of the essay.

3. DON'T write in clichés. Clichés include phrases like "all's well that ends well," "practice what you preach" and "it's a no-brainer." To you, phrases like these may seem clever. You may even use them regularly. But to admission officers, clichés are not only trite but they also reveal a lack of sophistication and originality. If you use clichés you will sound no better than a well-trained parrot. You want the admission officers to know that you are a capable writer who has the imagination and skill to write without the crutch of other people's overused phrases.

4. DON'T over quote. Along a similar vein as clichés, quotations also tend to make essays sound parrot like. In analytical essays, quotations are often a valuable component. However, in the limited space of the college essay, maintain your originality and don't allow quotations to distract from your voice.

Since quotations are not your own words, don't use them in a critical point or in place of your own analysis. Using a very well-known quotation is especially dangerous since many other applicants will almost certainly use similar quotations in their essays. If you want your essay to be memorable, it must be original. Put aside the *Bartlett's Book of Quotations* and start writing for yourself.

5. DON'T cross the line between creativity and absurdity. Most of the time the problem with admission essays is that they are not creative enough. However, some applicants, in an effort to insure that their essay is one-of-a-kind, go too far. Rather than sounding original and insightful, their essays appear trite and silly. A general rule is that you want your work to be as creative as possible but not so creative that admission officers won't take it seriously. If you have a question about whether your work crosses the line in the creativity department, get a second or third opinion. If one of your readers feels that the essay may be a little too off-the-wall, then tone it down or even abandon it. The college application is not the place to experiment and take radical chances. While you should write creatively, beware of the easy cross-over into silliness.

6. DON'T go thesaurus wild. Imagine the following tragic scene: ambulance lights are flashing, debris is scattered across the road and yellow police tape lines the highway. What happened? A terrible head-on collision between an essay and a thesaurus. It happens every year, and nearly every time the results are not pretty.

Writing your essay in the words of a thesaurus is one of the worst mistakes you can make. Many of the alternate words you find in a thesaurus will probably be unfamiliar to you. This means that if you use these alternate words, you run a high likelihood of using them awkwardly or incorrectly.

Admission officers possess a keen radar for picking out essays co-authored by a thesaurus. Call them psychic for this, but such essays really are not that hard to spot. Here is an excerpt from an essay that was definitely under the influence of the thesaurus:

> To recapitulate myself, I am an aesthetic and erudition-seeking personage. My superlative design in effervescence is to prospect divergent areas of the orb and to conceive these divergent cultures through the rumination of the lives of indisputable people.

This essay is the worst of its kind for using a thesaurus as a poor co-author. The author is clearly trying to impress, but has totally butchered correct word usage, not to mention common sense.

7. DON'T write a humorous essay if you are not humorous. Few people can write truly humorous essays, though thousands will try. Even if it may seem funny to you, all it takes is for one admission officer to be offended and you can kiss that letter of acceptance goodbye.

Unless you are a truly gifted humor writer, the test being that people other than yourself have said so, then stay away from the humorous essay. Think about stage comedians. Not everything they say is funny to everyone in the audience. Remember who your audience is and that your sense of humor is different from theirs. Untested humor is too difficult and unreliable to use in such a high-stakes essay.

8. DON'T resort to gimmicks. Applicants have written their essays in fluorescent highlighter or nail polish, sent cookies baked in the shape of the university's seal along with the essay and enclosed audio "mood" music that admission officers were supposed to play while reading their essays to create the right "ambiance." These tricks, while entertaining, are no substitute for substance.

While printing your essay in any other color than black is simply a bad idea from the point of view of readability, sending videos, audio tapes, computer programs and other multimedia is also usually a poor idea since they are often less impressive to admission officers than applicants may think.

9. DON'T write a sob story. Some students feel that they should catalog all the misfortunes and challenges that they have faced. While obstacles and family tragedies are appropriate topics, focusing on them without commenting on how you have grown or overcome those barriers will not make for a strong essay. While college admission officers are interested in obstacles, they are even more anxious to learn how you have excelled despite these challenges.

10. DON'T flex. For some strange reason, many applicants have a tendency to write about the great mysteries of the world or momentous philosophical debates in an effort to show admission officers their intelligence and sophistication. At Harvard we called people who wrote essays that aimed to impress rather than educate "flexors," as in people who flex their intellectual muscles.

While these essays attempt to present the illusion of sophistication, they are usually entirely without substance. Often they simply parrot back the opinions of others, and unless the writer is indeed knowledgeable about the subject, such essays are completely unoriginal.

College admission officers do not want to read an uninformed 17-year-old's diatribe on the nature of truth or the validity of Marxism. And

How Humor Can Kill An Essay

The dean of undergraduate admission at Case Western Reserve University recalls when humor failed

A humorous essay can be one of the best types to write. With a stack of essays to read, admission officers appreciate clever writing that makes them laugh. However, writing one of these essays is extremely difficult. Unless you have had experience with humor, we generally recommend that you don't rely on it to carry your essay.

William T. Conley, dean of undergraduate admission at Case Western Reserve University, always warns potential applicants to be cautious about using humor. Conley says, "Unfortunately a lot of adolescent humor can too often appear to be cynical, almost mean spirited even if unintentional. It's very hard to translate your humor from voice to paper. I've seen students succeed wonderfully because they can write humor effortlessly and others fail and fall flat on their face."

Conley recalls one incident where attempted humor totally bombed. He says, "I remember one essay where the student tried to be humorous and wrote about how smart he was and how he was smarter than all his teachers. Well, I used to be a teacher, and I wasn't laughing."

If you do attempt to write a humorous essay, be sure to have an adult read it and verify that it is funny. Remember that if you don't laugh at your parents' jokes, they probably don't laugh at yours either.

admission officers most certainly do not want to be lectured. Essays that try to impress with pseudo-intellectualism are definite candidates for the trash bin.

Remember the goal of the essay. Admission officers want to learn about the kind of person you are and the things that you have done. However, if your passion is reading Marx, then by all means write about it, but put it in perspective. Write about how you became interested in Marxism or its personal significance to you.

11. DON'T write a resume. A resume is the place where you detail your educational background, activities and jobs in terms of years of participation, titles and responsibilities. This should not be the topic of your college admission essay. Yet we have seen many students turn in essays that simply list their achievements like a resume, repeating information found elsewhere in the application and adding little if any insight.

12. DON'T try to second-guess what the admission officer wants to read. There are very few topics that you should avoid and there is absolutely no "correct" way to write an essay. Don't be afraid to try something unconventional and don't kill a good idea just because you think the admission officers wouldn't like it. If you care about your subject and it is important to you, the admission officers will appreciate your essay.

13. DON'T wait until the last minute. We have said before that the only way to test a topic is to write. We have emphasized that the only way to improve an essay is to keep re-writing. All of this requires time. One of the students who shared his essay in this book went through 20 drafts before he was finished. It took a lot of work, but his final product was worth the effort. The earlier you start writing the better. Plus, you want to make sure that you have time after your editors see your work to be able to make changes. Always allow yourself two to three times the time that you think it will take to write the essay.

14. DON'T generalize. Don't just say that you are a strong leader. Detail an example of when you've been a leader. Describe how you felt, what you did to motivate others and what you learned from the experience. Admission officers want details and examples from your life, not generalizations.

15. DON'T say it, show it. The best essays bring the readers into the middle of the action and help them see what the writer sees and hear what the writer hears. Appeal to the different senses. What can the reader see from your essay? Hear? Smell? (Hopefully nothing rotten.) The more you can draw the reader into your essay by using rich description the better.

16. DON'T get lazy with sentences. To write a truly memorable essay, each sentence needs to captivate the audience. That means that every sentence and each word in each sentence has to do its job of advancing the story or making a particular point. If you don't need a word or sentence get rid of it. Don't settle for a long, convoluted sentence when a shorter one will do. Be very disciplined and make every word count.

17. DON'T start the essay with "my name is." We don't usually dedicate a mistake to a specific phrase, but this one is used so often to start essays that we felt it necessary. Never, no matter what the circumstances, start your essay with this phrase. Spend the time to come up with a decent introduction.

18. DON'T use ghost writers. There is a disturbing trend of students hiring other people to write their essays. Not only is this unethical, but if you are caught (even after you are in college) you can expect immediate expulsion. While we encourage you to find people to edit your work and give you feedback, we absolutely reject the idea of anyone other than you writing your essay.

19. DON'T treat online applications like email. Written hastily and casually, most of the email we receive is full of errors. Unfortunately, when students submit their essays online there is a temptation to compose and submit their essays as if they were writing an email. This means the essays are not printed and proofread as carefully as they would be if submitted the old-fashioned way. If you are going to submit your essays online, be sure to print them out first and have other people edit your work. Treat essays submitted online as you would essays to be mailed.

20. DON'T assume specific knowledge. It is easy to forget that what you are familiar with may not be apparent to an admission officer. For example, you might write about the qualities of a new cartoon that everyone is talking about at your school. Everyone except the admission officer that is. Remember that you are a different generation. If you are writing about a teen idol, show or song you might want to add a one-sentence description for the benefit of those who may not be as familiar with it.

21. DON'T write a Hallmark card. Many essays written about family, grandparents or even history tend to be sentimentalized. This is because you respect these people and their deeds. However, praising family members or teachers and presenting their life and achievements as a tribute does not make an effective essay. It also shows a lack of critical analysis. We can all write glowing stories about our families, but it takes a more insightful person to write truthfully and even critically.

22. DON'T spill your guts. When we say that you need to reveal something about yourself we assume that it will be positive, be something that you are proud of and impress anybody reading it. You don't want to reveal secrets or write an exposé. Admission officers want to be impressed, not shocked or embarrassed. If what you are writing belongs in your diary then don't submit it to a college.

23. DON'T turn anything in without having at least one other person read it. It is vital to find people to read the essay and make comments. They will alert you to areas that are unclear and catch mistakes that you miss. Often their input is critical to the process of building a successful essay.

24. DON'T let your editors ruin your essay. There is one danger with editors. If you thoughtlessly incorporate every suggestion, you can end up destroying your essay. Keep in mind that you are the author and not every recommendation an editor makes may be necessary. You must agree with their opinions. You must remain in control or else your essay will lose its voice and focus.

25. DON'T end with a whimper. A powerful conclusion leaves readers with a strong impression of you. Try to end with something insightful or thought-provoking. Give the reader a memorable line or revelation that will stick with them after they put the essay down. And whatever you do, don't abruptly end your essay with the words "THE END."

The Importance Of Editors

Nothing is more critical to creating a successful essay than having editors. Very few students have written a strong essay without some help and input from others. Plus, editors will catch embarrassing mistakes that you may miss after reading your essay for the 24th time.

Get friends, teachers and family to read your essays. Some editors are skilled at catching spelling and grammatical mistakes, while others are great at providing suggestions on content. You need both kinds of editors. Ideally, editors will help identify areas of your essay that are confusing or unnecessary. They can give feedback on the essay's structure and whether or not the transitions work. They can also comment on your main idea and how well it is conveyed.

If you plan on using humor, get an adult to double check what you (and perhaps your friends) think is funny. Remember you might get an admission officer who does not appreciate the humor of the Simpsons or South Park.

Getting editorial feedback is not easy on the ego since someone may tear apart work that you have spent days creating. However, view all criticism as constructive and know that it will help you to craft a stronger essay, which in turn will help you get into college, which is, after all, your primary goal.

The one danger to avoid is that you should not blindly accept every suggestion. Remember that you are the author and you need to filter your editor's suggestions and act upon those that make sense to you. If you just insert everyone's comments into your essay, you will ruin it. It will become unfocused and your voice will be lost.

Make sure that while you welcome feedback from others you keep their comments in perspective and only use those that you feel will improve your essay. In the end you are the captain of your essay. While your editors provide valuable support, you are still responsible for its ultimate destination.

CHAPTER FIVE

RECYCLING YOUR ESSAYS

In this chapter you will learn:

- Why the Common Application is the ideal way to recycle

- How to save time by modifying one essay to submit to many colleges

- Warnings about recycling

Don't Throw Away A Good Essay

After a workshop we gave on essay writing, a student approached us with a bewildered look. He said, "I understand the importance of a good essay, and I even have some ideas. But I'm planning to apply to a lot of colleges, and I don't think I can write that many good essays."

Fortunately, we reassured him that he would not have to dedicate the next six months of his life to writing essays. The solution to his problem is recycling.

Recycling has nothing to do with aluminum cans (although we encourage that type of recycling as well) but everything to do with saving time. After all, why go through the difficult and time-consuming essay-writing process again and again to answer each school's essay questions when you can often modify a few essays to answer all of them? Most students find that if they write just a handful of good essays, they have enough to answer an almost unlimited number of questions.

The Common Application: The Best Way To Recycle

The ultimate in recycling is to mail the same essay word for word to all the colleges to which you are applying. While a fantasy for past applicants, this is increasingly becoming a reality through the growing acceptance of the Common Application.

The Common Application is a single application that over 275 schools accept in place of their own application. This means that if you are applying to more than one school that accepts the Common Application, you can send the same exact application to each of these schools. Get more information on the Common Application at www.commonapp. org. Note that some schools that accept the Common Application require their own supplemental forms.

And for those schools that do not accept the Common Application, which unfortunately is still the majority, you will need to learn the art of recycling.

Modifying An Existing Essay

The key to recycling is that most colleges ask you the same underlying question, which is to tell them something important about yourself. Even if at first the questions appear different, for the most part the answers can be the same. Often, changing the introduction and conclusion and doing some editing of the body are all that is needed to recycle an essay.

Let's look at an example of how this might work. A typical essay question is, "Evaluate a significant experience or achievement that has special meaning to you." Since you are a smart applicant who has read this book, you would follow all the tips in the previous chapters and after several weeks have a perfect essay describing, for example, a hike in the Grand Canyon that changed your outlook on life. This essay directly addresses the significant experience question and could be mailed as is.

However, for another school, you might think you need to write an entirely new essay to answer their question, "Describe a book, class, project or person that you find intellectually exciting."

Before you begin brainstorming, wait a minute. If you have read any books along the lines of *Robinson Crusoe*, *Tom Sawyer*, *Huckleberry Finn* or *The Heart of Darkness*, you could in your introduction begin by referring to one of these books, describing the importance of nature and adventure in the book and then showing how these same themes have affected your life.

With a good transition, you could then attach word for word the main body of your first essay describing your own adventure in the Grand Canyon and how it changed your views. In the conclusion you could again juxtapose your adventure with that of one of the characters or themes in the novel and reemphasize the significance of both the book and adventure in your life.

The result would be another perfect essay that only took a fraction of the time to write. The major requirement for recycling to be successful is that you have at least one good essay with which to begin.

Remember that as powerful as recycling is, it will not improve a bad essay. In fact, a bad essay recycled and sent to 100 schools will still only yield 100 rejections.

A Final Warning About Recycling

The greatest danger of recycling is that in the process of clipping and reworking, the original focus of your essay can be lost. To make sure that this does not happen, reread the question and your essay several times. Ask yourself: Does this essay truly answer the question? Remember that while you have the freedom to interpret the question in your own way, you do not want the admission officers to wonder if you misunderstood it because your essay lacks focus and does not clearly state at the beginning how you intend to answer the question.

Here are some other important questions to ask yourself:

- Does the introduction set up the essay so that it is clear that you are trying to answer the stated question?
- Have you given too much or too little information or detail?
- Do the sentences and paragraphs flow together well?
- Are the transitions smooth and the connections between your ideas apparent?
- Is the logic of the essay preserved?

If you are unsure about your recycled work, get a second opinion. Have someone who has not read the original essay read the recycled essay to see if it is still clear and understandable.

Although recycling can produce an essay in a fraction of the time, careful attention still needs to be exercised especially when writing the introduction and conclusion. Your recycled work needs to be just as polished as the original essay. When you are done, congratulate yourself on having saved valuable time and effort.

CHAPTER SIX

ROUNDTABLE WITH ADMISSION OFFICERS

In this chapter you will learn:

- **What happens to your essay after it arrives in the admission office**

- **Why the admission process is subjective**

- **The real reason why colleges require essays**

- **What impresses admission officers**

- **Common essay mistakes that students make year after year**

- **What you might be surprised to learn about your essay**

- **Advice on what makes a successful essay**

Meet The Admission Officers

Water is always fresher the closer you are to the source. In this chapter we head right to the source and ask admission officers—point blank—what they are looking for in your essays. After having seen thousands and even tens of thousands of essays, these admission officers offer invaluable insight into the admission process. We asked them what works, what mistakes they hope you will avoid and what advice they have for writing the essay.

QUESTION:

Can you give students an idea of what happens to their applications and essays after they are received by your college?

ANSWER:

Peter Osgood
Director of Admission, Harvey Mudd College
Former Associate Dean of Admission, Pomona College
First, we collect all the different parts of the application. Once everything is assembled we start to read them one by one. Unlike many colleges, we don't sort the applications into regional categories. They are placed into completely random groups.

Once you've read one application folder you pass it on to someone else who will also review it. We read and then read some more. After reading all the applications we'll start meeting and discussing the merits of each applicant one by one.

We don't only look at the applicants at the top end of some academic or extracurricular scale. Every single application is reviewed through this process. There's a lot of yapping among admission officers. I have a placard in my office that says a lot about the process, "When all is said and done, more will be said than done."

Gail Sweezey
Director of Admissions, Gettysburg College

All applications are reviewed once and then put into a file. Then we review them a second, third and even fourth time. We look at a student's academic record and actually examine the student's senior year first. While we like to see A's and B's, we also look at the level of competition and difficulty of the high school. We are keenly aware that schools have different grading scales. We review SAT or ACT scores within the context of the academic record. We also look carefully at recommendations, extracurricular activities both in school and outside of school and, of course, the essay.

William T. Conley
Dean of Undergraduate Admission, Case Western Reserve University

We have nine professional admission counselors who are assigned specific geographic areas. We break the country down so that each counselor can travel to the schools in their region and understand the nature of the community. This system reassures students that their application is being read by a person who can appreciate that application within the correct context.

Each admission counselor reviews their region's applications and makes initial recommendations. Then everything is forwarded to me. I am the second reader for all applications. I ultimately sign off on every student that we admit. If I don't agree with the counselor's initial recommendation then the application goes back to the counselor and we may bring in a third reader. If we still cannot agree, then the application goes to a committee, which includes members of the faculty. About 15 percent of all our applications will need to be decided upon by the committee.

Lloyd Peterson
Former Senior Associate Director of Admissions, Yale University
Director of Education, College Coach Inc.

At Yale everyone in the office is assigned a geographic region. The application is really a dense document. Every application will get a minimum of two readings. If you applied for early decision and were deferred you would get three readings. International students also usually get an extra read.

Sometimes after two readings one reader says, "This applicant is a clear admit." But a second reader says, "Are you crazy?" That's when we bring in a third reader. If you're surprised by this, you should remember that we are all individuals. We are all human. Many times two admission officers will see the same candidate differently.

Michael Thorp
Director of Admissions, Lawrence University
An application is first read by a counselor responsible for a geographical territory. We do this so that the counselor knows something about the schools and cities in their area. Once the counselor has read the application and made his or her decision, all applications are given to me. I do the final reading and approve the counselor's recommendations. We spend a lot of time reading each piece of the application. Many people assume that this level of attention given to each application can only happen at smaller colleges like ours. Students often don't believe that we will read every piece of paper that they submit. We do. We spend many long days reading applications.

Elizabeth Mosier
Acting Director of Admissions, Bryn Mawr College
Compared to many colleges, our process is more labor-intensive. We have a committee made up of current students, admission officers and faculty members. We divide this group into subcommittees that are responsible for specific geographic areas. Therefore, every file is read multiple times and is then discussed in the committee.

Each member of the committee is extremely important. The students know the college well. They've experienced not only what it's like to make the transition from high school to college but they also have a perspective on the workload and what each applicant may be able to contribute to the Bryn Mawr community. The faculty knows most about the classes and what it takes for a student to thrive academically. We try to have the faculty represent a broad range of interests. The admission officers are often the applicant's advocate in terms of knowing about their specific high school and region. We're the experts on how high schools compare to one another.

Basically, from mid-November to mid-March we're wearing sweat pants, drinking lots of coffee and reading folders. It's very intense but also a lot of fun.

QUESTION:

Many students are surprised at how subjective the admission process can be. Why is it not a completely numbers-based, objective process?

ANSWER:

Peter Osgood
Director of Admission, Harvey Mudd College
Former Associate Dean of Admission, Pomona College

At Harvey Mudd our selection process is highly individualized. The reason is because the vast majority of applicants present very similar records in terms of SAT scores and GPAs. Most fall within the top 10 percent of their high school classes. Using these objective criteria or the marginal differences in a student's GPA doesn't serve us or the students very well.

The kinds of things that tend to be intriguing to us and may even suggest potential for real success here are qualities like attitudes toward learning, problem-solving ability and being able to work with others. In other words, qualities that objective measurements are not good at measuring. Intellectual curiosity, for example, doesn't necessarily translate into a particular grade. Since we look for these other qualities, the essay is one area where we expect to find them.

Lloyd Peterson
Former Senior Associate Director of Admissions, Yale University
Director of Education, College Coach Inc.

At Yale, when we assembled the various parts of the application into a folder we put all the qualitative pieces, like the essay, up front. The reason is because I wanted to get to know the applicant as an individual before I saw the numbers like their GPA and SAT scores. I wanted to know John Smith the person before I knew John Smith the scholar. That's why I always looked at the essays and recommendations first. If I looked at an SAT score first, it would have too much influence on the rest of my reading. I didn't want to go into the essay thinking 1280. I want a blank canvas. This philosophy is very typical at the Ivy League and other selective schools.

Elizabeth Mosier
Acting Director of Admissions, Bryn Mawr College
Many applicants imagine the admission committee meetings as taking place in a smoke-filled room with a bunch of sneaky people looking for any reason not to admit them. I hate to disappoint anyone, but the committee meetings are actually quite congenial. We discuss each candidate. We don't always agree, and sometimes we can debate for hours. But this is all part of what makes our process work.

Because we are a small college and have the ability to evaluate each applicant individually, we can be really focused on the match between the applicant and our campus. We try to ask ourselves if the applicant would thrive in this environment. It's not an exact science admitting students. It's a very personal process. If students can write essays that show us who they want to be, that helps us see them in our college. We want to make good matches. We want students to come here and love it.

QUESTION:

Many students wonder why colleges require an essay. What is the real reason for the essay?

ANSWER:

Lloyd Peterson
Former Senior Associate Director of Admissions, Yale University
Director of Education, College Coach Inc.
College admission for the most part is a two-dimensional process. It is the essays that add the vital third dimension. We don't want to know your family history or what we can learn from your application or transcript. We use the essays as a window into your soul. We want to see a slice of your life that is the most meaningful to you.

William T. Conley
Dean of Undergraduate Admission, Case Western Reserve University
The essay is one of the means that we use to validate other information and achievements. For instance, if an applicant is an A student in English and we read an essay that's fundamentally flawed, then we would question whether or not the transcript tells an accurate story. On the

other hand we might have an applicant who has a C in English but who produces a beautiful essay. It might alert us to the fact that this applicant doesn't "march to the same drum" as other students at his school but is nevertheless a brilliant writer. Upon investigating further we may discover that the real question we need to ask about this applicant is whether or not we want a brilliant writer who may sleep through 8 a.m. classes. Students need to take the essay seriously. It's not the only part of your application, but don't underestimate it either.

Michael Thorp
Director of Admissions, Lawrence University
The essay is important because we can't interview every student who applies. The essay is the students' chance to let us get to know them as an individual. It helps the students become more than a transcript and test score. It helps us empathize with who they are. It also helps us know how well the students can organize their thoughts into coherent sentences and paragraphs.

Most admission people are looking for reasons to admit you—even at schools that admit a very small percentage of their applicants. You may have a 4.0 and 1600 SAT, but so do thousands of other students. This is where the essay comes in and where we can see the students' unique perspective and personality.

Elizabeth Mosier
Acting Director of Admissions, Bryn Mawr College
The essay is important. The essay is where we in the admission committee get to learn more about each applicant and see what they believe in and value. Because writing itself is a way of demonstrating your ability to think, we get a good idea of how a student thinks through the essay. For many people an admission essay may just look like another piece of paper, but to us it is a window into an applicant's mind.

Gail Sweezey
Director of Admissions, Gettysburg College
While the essay is part of the overall package, and we do look carefully at everything, it does offer students the best chance for reflection. For us in the admission office it is our best chance to learn what is important to the applicant. From their essays we can see what they value.

QUESTION:

Let's get to the heart of the matter. What are the qualities of a successful admission essay? What impresses you when you read an essay?

ANSWER:

Peter Osgood
Director of Admission, Harvey Mudd College
Former Associate Dean of Admission, Pomona College

Contrary to popular belief, we are not really looking to be entertained. What we want is to see that the applicant has done some serious thinking and reflection. I am looking for a certain amount of thought to have been put into the essay. When we ask, "Tell us who you are," that's exactly what we want to know.

Perspective is also something that I look for in essays. It's hard for high school seniors to remove themselves from the daily grind and be able to step back and write something that's meaningful. However, those who can usually end up with powerful essays.

Gail Sweezey
Director of Admissions, Gettysburg College

When I read an essay, I expect it to be structured appropriately. That means that the essay must have a beginning, middle and end. But most important it must have a thesis that is developed throughout the essay.

While we want students to explore themselves through their essays and take some chances in their writing, we also expect that they spend the time to edit their work. As I always advise students, the best essays are written from the heart, but proofread from the head.

William T. Conley
Dean of Undergraduate Admission, Case Western Reserve University

The essay needs to be in your own words. We need to hear your voice and get a genuine sense that you are writing about what matters to you. I think that's where many students get off track. They answer the question but they do so in a manner that seems too stilted or artificial. One of my favorite questions years ago was when we asked students to name a book they read that had a great impact on them. It was a simple but deadly question because a lot of students felt that they had to select a significant book like *War & Peace*. Students would submit essays about these impressive-sounding titles and then reflect on them in a simplistic way that told us nothing about them. On the other hand, I still remember a student writing about *The Little Engine That Could*. It was brilliant since she used the story to reflect on her life and gave vivid, memorable examples.

Michael Thorp
Director of Admissions, Lawrence University
I look for a unique perspective on something the student has done. If you look at the tone of essay questions out there, you will notice how general the topics are. This is simply the students' chance to show us how well they think and how well they can communicate with the written word.

I also personally like humor. There is nothing I would appreciate more at 11 p.m. after picking up the 150th essay than for it to make me chuckle. Of course, if you're not funny, now's not the time to experiment.

Something that I am not looking for is a tell-all. Sometimes student feel the need to tell me something very personal about their life. That's okay as long as I'm not the first person they've told. I don't need to know their deepest, darkest secrets. Students should be aware of who is reading their essay. We're not a professor, we're not their best friend, we're not a political correspondent. We are admission folk. There are a lot of things that admission people share such as the fact that we all want to find out something good about each applicant. Students should think about who we are and make sure their essay is appropriate for us.

Lloyd Peterson
Former Senior Associate Director of Admissions, Yale University
Director of Education, College Coach Inc.
I once calculated that I've read about 42,000 essays in my career. One crucial fact that I learned is that while you have to answer the question, you also have to understand what the question is asking. Unless

you sit down and think about it before you start writing you're going to miss the boat.

One year I read 18 essays in a row about Gandhi. I know more about Gandhi than I want to know. The problem was that Gandhi was not applying for admission. The students were. Each of those students forgot that what I wanted to learn was something about them. They neglected to write about their reaction to Gandhi or include comparisons to their own thought process and values. Students need to take a stand and voice an opinion. When the admission officer finishes your essay, they should know something important about you—not Gandhi.

Elizabeth Mosier
Acting Director of Admissions, Bryn Mawr College
The best essays use dramatic elements like dialogue and interesting narrative. You really want the admission officer to get hooked into your essay. We all respond to good narrative. It's a compelling way to tell a story.

Applicants should remember that we are not looking for you to write about a spectacular achievement. You don't have to find the cure for cancer at age 17. Sometimes even small events can be great subjects. One student talked about her work for a pro-choice organization that she thought was going to be a profound experience but instead she had to dress up as a condom elf. What we're really hoping to see in the essay is that the student is thinking beyond her own limited experience. Even if it seems small, you have experienced something. You will be profound.

QUESTION:

What common mistakes do students make on essays year after year? How can they avoid these mistakes?

ANSWER:

Peter Osgood
Director of Admission, Harvey Mudd College
Former Associate Dean of Admission, Pomona College
Sometimes students hear that certain essays work and try to copy them. What they end up with is a contrived essay that appears to have been forced to fit the student. This just doesn't work. You need to write your own essay that is special and unique to you. My other big complaint: two-page essays with no paragraphs.

Gail Sweezey
Director of Admissions, Gettysburg College
Sometimes I think too many adults get involved with rewriting a student's essay. It's important to have someone look at your essay, but they should not try to substantially change it. What happens then is that the student's voice is lost.

Michael Thorp
Director of Admissions, Lawrence University
One mistake is to let your assumptions about the reader be the primary guide for your essay. A student will assume that because the school I work for is conservative that I'm conservative too. Don't make specific assumptions about your audience. I don't care if a student writes about a conservative or liberal topic as long as it's framed within the context of what the student has done. When students write that they should be admitted by virtue of their conservative values, that is not a compelling reason to admit them. I don't care if a student is a member of the John Birch Society as long as she articulates why that's important to her.

Lloyd Peterson
Former Senior Associate Director of Admissions, Yale University
Director of Education, College Coach Inc.
Having too many editors and too many people with their hands in the mix. If too many people try to change an essay you often don't know whose voice it is. The other big mistake is to submit an essay that earned you an A+ in English or History class. Often these essays do not make good admission essays.

Elizabeth Mosier
Acting Director of Admissions, Bryn Mawr College
One mistake is not being original enough. Don't write about what everyone else will write about. For example, the school shooting at Columbine is a really important topic but it's also difficult to say anything original about it. Basically, with so many people using it for their essays it has a built-in disadvantage. A really good writer may be able to pull it off, but for most students choosing this as a topic is a recipe for failure.

Another example is when students are asked to write a character portrait. The grandmother essay is hard to resist. I think the problem with writing about a grandparent is not the topic but the fact that the topic is fraught with the danger to sentimentalize and not reveal the truth. Most of these essays end up being something that is like a Hallmark card. Grandparents can be a great topic as long as you have something original and unique to say.

QUESTION:

What are some things that students might be surprised to learn about how you read their essays?

ANSWER:

Peter Osgood
Director of Admission, Harvey Mudd College
Former Associate Dean of Admission, Pomona College
I think students would be surprised to know that while we are required to evaluate them, we are truly interested in what experiences have

affected their thoughts and values. I know that students sometimes think, "They can't possibly know me, how dare they judge me." I can understand that, but at least through the essay we are giving students an opportunity to share something significant. We appreciate any student who makes the attempt to try to reveal to us something about them.

Gail Sweezey
Director of Admissions, Gettysburg College
I think students would be surprised by how interested we are in their story. We take all submissions very seriously and use them to get to know each applicant better.

William T. Conley
Dean of Undergraduate Admission, Case Western Reserve University
About 40 percent of our incoming class is engineers. For them to write a powerful and persuasive essay is more difficult than someone who's going to major in English or history. While that is not an excuse, we do take into account that for some students the writing component will not be their strength and we will evaluate their essay in proportion to their other strengths. But it would be a grave mistake for these students to think that getting an 800 on their math SAT means that their essays don't count. That is totally wrong. We still need to see effort. We want to see that they gave it their best shot.

Michael Thorp
Director of Admissions, Lawrence University
They might be surprised to learn that indeed good writing matters. Sometimes students think that there's some kind of magic formula. If they can just find the most unique topic that exists they will have the perfect essay. But the truth is that it's not the topic but the writing that matters.

Lloyd Peterson
Former Senior Associate Director of Admissions, Yale University
Director of Education, College Coach Inc.
I think some students are surprised to know how dangerous it is to second-guess what the admission officer would like to read. I have

read about everything imaginable: secret marriages, kleptomania and pyromania. Each was trying to create shock value, and it just didn't work. Don't second-guess us. Write about what you care about.

You also hear that you should never write about the Two D's: divorce and death. Poppycock. If your parents' divorce has had an impact on you and you can write about it in an impassioned way, then write about it. And I have read a lot of grandmother essays in my time. But that should not stop you from writing about your grandmother since I haven't read *your* grandmother essay.

Elizabeth Mosier
Acting Director of Admissions, Bryn Mawr College
I think students would be surprised to learn that we're not looking for a particular Bryn Mawr prototype. We're looking for someone to be a contributor. We really want to admit you, and we look to your essay and application to give us a reason to do so. Admission officers like students. We wouldn't be in this business unless we liked working with students. We're hoping that you'll make us forget that it's an essay and just impress us with your unique talents and interests.

QUESTION

In your career, you have read thousands if not tens of thousands of essays. What advice do you have for students?

ANSWER:

Lloyd Peterson
Former Senior Associate Director of Admissions, Yale University
Director of Education, College Coach Inc.
In today's admission marketplace the essay can move you up and down the scale. A strong essay can make a difference. The most important thing you can do to improve your writing is to constantly rewrite. Work on perfecting your essay. Don't pull an all-nighter and think that is enough to produce a successful essay. You need to spend time on each essay every day. Rewriting is more important than the first draft. Writing isn't easy. You need to work at it. You can't treat it like a midterm

exam and do it all the night before. You need to bite the bullet and work your tail off to create a compelling essay.

Elizabeth Mosier
Acting Director of Admissions, Bryn Mawr College
I suggest that you start with an oral draft. Tell your story to a friend. Tell it to a parent. That will get you started. You learn what you believe, what you value and what kind of people you admire. Plus, who better than a friend to say, "Oh please, you're full of it." Writing your essay should be a process, just like discussing an idea, and it should bring you to a place you've never been before.

William T. Conley
Dean of Undergraduate Admission, Case Western Reserve University
I tell students to start thinking as early as their sophomore or junior years about what they've read, stories they've heard and events in their life that even if they were simple events had huge implications for them. We're really jaded when it comes to essays and topics. We've read the ones about visiting the Wailing Wall or standing at the top of the Eiffel Tower. Sometimes it's as if the student feels the only way to stand out is by being the only survivor of the Titanic. But we really appreciate someone writing about a simple incident and showing us a deeper meaning. Think about your friendships, your disappointments, your successes and the basics in life. If you do this early, you will have a wealth of options to write about when the time comes.

Peter Osgood
Director of Admission, Harvey Mudd College
Former Associate Dean of Admission, Pomona College
The essay is usually the last thing the student does. They put it off until the very end. This creates a lot of problems. A lot of students in my opinion try to make themselves into their vision of what the colleges want. If the student has done a good search and started from inside themselves and then found colleges that match them, they have less to worry about. We sometimes get these hyper, anxious students who are trying to conform themselves to what they think the college wants. Students should work inside out and their essays should be an extension of that.

Gail Sweezey
Director of Admissions, Gettysburg College
I always remind students that the application is really a way to tell their story. Think of the essay as a piece of your story and then tell it to us.

CHAPTER SEVEN

57 SUCCESSFUL ADMISSION ESSAYS

In this chapter you will read essays on:

- **Personal beliefs & reflections**
- **Influential books**
- **Family**
- **Influential people**
- **Things that represent me**
- **Writing essays**
- **Extracurricular activities & athletics**
- **Music**
- **Math & science**
- **Jobs & careers**
- **Issues**
- **Overcoming a weakness or challenge**
- **Places**

Learn from 57 Successful Essays

One of the most difficult things we have learned (some would say we are still learning) was how to train our dog. While we read how-to books on dog training and got advice from friends, the most useful teaching aid turned out to be a video. It was effective because it actually showed dogs learning the commands. It gave us a chance to see how a well-trained dog was supposed to behave (which helped since we had not witnessed such behavior in our own dog.) The visual examples in the video gave us a goal to aim toward and confidence that a dog could learn the new tricks.

In the same spirit of training, we present 57 successful admission essays so you, too, can see how the lessons in the previous chapters are put into action. (Yes, the title of this book promises 50 essays, but being overachievers, we decided to give you more!) As you write your own masterpiece, use these as inspiration and models to compare to your own work.

But before you start, a modest warning. These are by no means the only ways to write a successful essay. In fact, these essays worked because they reflected the writers' unique experiences, achievements, thoughts and personality. Your own background and style are no doubt different and therefore your essays will be different.

Use these to understand the qualities that make a successful essay. Analyze each and understand why it is interesting and memorable and ultimately helped the writer get accepted. Look at the use of language. Appreciate how the writers approach their subjects. Try to uncover their motivations. In other words, learn from these examples, and be inspired by them. But whatever you do, don't try to copy them.

We guarantee that if you follow the strategies in the previous chapters and infuse your own personality and way of thinking into your writing, you, too, can produce a powerful and effective essay that is all your own.

Now, let's read some successful essays.

Personal Beliefs and Reflections

Jessica Haskins
Saratoga Springs, New York

Jessica is not one to hide what she really cares about in her writing. For her college applications, she wrote about Dr. Seuss, becoming an atheist and *Star Trek*. She advises, "If you let your own personality come through, your essay will be much more powerful and striking." At Saratoga Springs High School, she avidly wrote in a heavy load of AP courses and by keeping a daily diary and nightly dream journal. In the future, she hopes to use her "wild imagination" in fantasy novels and short stories.

IDIC, Anyone?
Bard College

All right, I'm going to do it. I'm going to write an essay about *Star Trek*.

I hope you haven't read many *Star Trek* essays before this one. They tend to be formulaic, lauding Trek's vision of a brighter, better future, its daring in employing a multiethnic cast, its inspiring mission "to boldly go"... I think all that stuff is cool too, but everything about it has already been said, and I don't want to add to the mountain of pages already written on those subjects. I'll attempt to come up with something marginally more original by discussing a different facet of Trek, one that has had a larger impact on me personally.

I understand that you may have never seen an episode of *Star Trek* in your life. You may be thinking, "Isn't that the one with the guy with the funny ears?" You *may* be thinking, "Isn't that the one with that Yoda guy?", but I hope not. (That's *Star Wars*, by the by.) I'm going to talk about the people with the "funny ears," people who I think are rather neat. They're called Vulcans, and they live according to a philosophy called IDIC. (Aha! I remember that word from the title! But what does it mean?)

"IDIC" stands for "Infinite Diversity in Infinite Combinations." It is the Vulcan national symbol and one of their highest principles. What it means is that we should respect everyone and everything in the universe, and appreciate, rather than attempt to eradicate, their differences. At the core of this concept there is also a sense of awe at the beauty and complexity of the universe and consequently a deep reluctance to corrupt it by forcing conformity upon naturally diverse elements. Another way to sum it up is with this quote from Surak, the "father of Vulcan philosophy": "Any given group is far more than the sum of its infinite parts, and the parts all infinitely less for the loss of one of them." This philosophy of recognizing value in everyone, even those who may disagree with you, is an appealing one that I've strived to embrace.

The more oft-remarked-upon characteristic of Vulcans is their strict adherence to the principles of logic. Vulcans eschew outward displays of emotion, preferring to reason out a situation instead of reacting instinctively. The discipline of choosing logic over emotion is called *cthia*, though the name is not commonly known. I've seen people around me react to problems irrationally, maybe snapping at someone in a moment of anger, blaming them for something that wasn't their fault. They'll regret the words later, but *cthia* is a reminder to me to think before I speak, to consider the effect my words and actions will have on other people.

The ideas I've mentioned so far are the lessons to which I refer most often. Vulcans have much more to recommend them: They are pacifists, vegetarians, philosophers and scientists. They value knowledge and learning above almost all else. They have a saying: "The spear in the other's heart is the spear in your own. You are he." They are very empathic, determined to "ideally, do no harm." They are at peace with the world.

That is why I have adopted the Vulcans as role models. I believe that we look for teachers to teach us the lessons we're convinced we need to learn, and Vulcan characters in *Star Trek* are very convenient teachers, modeling the way I'd like to view and fit into the world. Watching them hasn't defined my way of thinking, but it has influenced it and helped me to define it a little better myself. They say that the best way to tell the truth is through fiction.

And I've just got to say it: Live long and prosper.

Why This Essay Succeeded

Even though you've never met her, can't you just picture what Jessica may be like? Doesn't her essay convey her personality through the description of what she finds so appealing about the Vulcan philosophy? Essays that leave the readers with a clearer idea of who the writer is are always good. While Jessica's essay at first appears to be an analysis of *Star Trek*, it's really a portrait of herself.

Throughout the essay Jessica doesn't just describe, she analyzes. Colleges want students who are introspective, who can take a step back from their own lives and examine them. Instead of merely reporting the values she has learned from the Vulcans, Jessica interprets why these values (which are, after all, from a fictional people) are important to her and how they affect her. It's clear that Jessica has thought a lot about the deeper philosophical themes of this television show.

Finally, who wouldn't admire Jessica's bravery for admitting that she is a "Trekkie?" Most people imagine a "Trekkie" as a dork without a life. But Jessica unapologetically and proudly admits her love for *Star Trek* and convinces us that even if we are not fans of the show that we, too, can learn something from the underlying message of the show's characters. And Jessica is certainly not a dork.

Sameer H. Doshi

Toronto, Canada

Sameer wrote this essay after a family dinner party one night; a long but pleasant day in the kitchen helped him reflect on what he hoped to accomplish in college. He grew up in suburban Detroit until his family moved to Toronto when he was in high school. Sameer tried to stay busy at his new high school, A.Y. Jackson Secondary. His favorite activities were cross country, debate and his school newspaper, *The Core.* Sameer is color-blind and tone-deaf, which he says explains why his creative expression is limited to cooking! He hopes to be an advocate for environmental policy.

Culinary Creation
Harvard University

My aim is creation. I love the idea of giving life to nothingness. Were I another person in another time, I might spend my whole life tilling the land. Just like the earliest farmers, the sight of dirt giving rise to carrots and tomatoes at my whim feels like a miracle. I like to randomly burst out in song. I like to shake my body. If I could I would be a pianist and a poet and a painter and a politician. Unfortunately, in all these disciplines my ability can't meet my enthusiasm. Where I can create, and break tired codes, is in the kitchen. With unlimited time and resources I would become the best pastry baker and the finest chef in all of the eastern seaboard.

I really like food. On some drab school days I cheer myself up thinking of the dinner awaiting me in the evening. Often I do a 24-hour fast to ready my stomach for a huge meal. Now, being served this food is fine. It's usually restful and rewarding to sit down after a long day to someone else's careful work, whether they be parents, grandmothers or Little Caesar. But I've noticed a dull glaze in the eyes of those who cook every night. They're doing it not to forge the uncreated conscience of their race, as a hungry James Joyce might say, but out of sometimes love and sometimes duty. I know cooks whose "old standbys" wow me every time, but they haven't any pleasure in their labors. Care and duty are NOT why I want to explore food.

I love the whole culinary process, from seedling to grocery to refrigerator to oven to table. At each stage the elements grow more complex and my work far more deliberate. Peeling and coring an apple takes more intellection than planting a row of seeds. Yet I think I shine where order fades away: beyond rules and recipes, in that zone called It's Up To You. I decided to throw in a cup of yogurt instead of butter to my pound cake. No one told me that lentils, carrots and a bay leaf would make a great salad. I just felt them together. And there was a unanimous vote—me—to add cumin and coriander to the spaghetti sauce. Sizzle. Bubble. The creation is imminent

Someone like me needs to stand over that stove. I need to see the joy in my eaters' eyes when they say, "This is really good! How'd you do this?" Their simple joys are my creative release—the critical acceptance of newness. In life and in the kitchen, I want to be the best in my field.

Why This Essay Succeeded

Since he is writing about cooking, it's not surprising that Sameer's essay appeals to the senses. From his word choice and sentence structure, you can see the carrots and tomatoes ripening, smell the coriander and cumin simmering and almost taste the lentil salad. These sensual cues help to make his essay jump from the page.

But Sameer's essay is not just a tasty recipe. Sameer explains why he loves cooking and how it gives him a level of freedom to create that is beyond what he can experience in the other areas of his life. He makes it clear that his approach to perfection in cooking is also the same approach he takes to life.

Sameer's essay is an excellent example of blending descriptive language with poignant analysis that is a joy to read and leaves our mouth watering for more.

Elisa Tatiana Juárez

Miami, Florida

Based on her research in osteoporosis and gerontology, Elisa has won awards in a number of competitions including the Intel International Science and Engineering Fair and the South Florida Science and Engineering Fair. But each time she entered a competition, she noticed that economically disadvantaged students were underrepresented. She did something to change this. Working with the Miami Museum of Science and Big Brothers Big Sisters, she founded the Students and Teachers Advocating Research Science (STARS) program to assist disadvantaged middle school children. A graduate of Coral Reef Senior High, Elisa has been recognized for her work and won both the Hispanic Heritage Youth Award and the Target All-Around Scholarship.

Birks and Barbie
Brown University

I am not a Barbie doll.

I came to that realization the day I discovered the power of Birkenstocks. As we all know, Barbie is genetically engineered by marketing professionals to wear stiletto heels every day of her life, which makes it impossible for her to even consider Birkenstocks. On the other hand, I have molded my Birkenstocks to my feet. To put my feet into a pair of five-inch spikes would be criminal. This whole concept is quite simple actually. Here let me explain. Which of the "new and improved" Barbie dolls stands up against all odds and wins international science awards? Or walks through the streets of México teaching children Bible stories? Or spends her Saturdays in downtown Miami feeding homeless people? How many times have you heard of Barbie advocating the rights of women and minorities? Never, as far as I know.

When I was younger I never had a Barbie doll. There was something about her that I just didn't like. Growing up, I remember getting chemistry and biology kits as gifts, not a plastic doll with long blonde hair and beyond-perfect measurements. Now, don't get me wrong, Barbie is a wonderful inspiration to many of us. She teaches wonderful marketing skills, she stands for the capitalism America is known for; whether or not that is a good thing is up to you. Still, I was very disappointed when I dissected a neighbor's Barbie one day and discovered that there was nothing inside. She was empty, hollow, uninteresting scientifically, and I soon lost interest.

I mentioned that Barbie does not wear Birkenstocks. How would that help you learn more about me? When I slip on a pair of Birks I feel invincible. I think it has to do with the stories my mother told me growing up. Protesting against the Vietnam War, wearing flowers in her hair and fighting for peace, all the while sporting leather sandals. Those stories have been an inspiration to me. She made me think of all the things that I was capable of doing. She was the one who gave me my first pair of Birks and planted in them was the power of invincibility. To this day I wear my Birkenstocks to everything I do that is non-conventional. I tend to look at life outside the box, unlike Barbie, whose imagination and very existence depends on the plastic box that surrounds her.

Never once in my life did I imagine that I would compete one day against the best high school science projects in the world. Through my perseverance, tenacity and faith in myself, I was able to not only fulfill my dream, but also to do more. Due to my success in science fairs internationally, I began to sense that it was not fair that other kids weren't given the same opportunities. This motivated me to start a project involving middle and elementary school age children from economically disadvantaged backgrounds to come together and create with exciting projects. The goal of this project is to give kids confidence in science. So what if they come from "disadvantaged" backgrounds? They should have the same opportunities as others. The group of kids I am working with now is small, but they are so excited about science and research. Just the other day, one of my girls came up to me and said, "I don't really like science, my thing is literature and English, but these workshops have given me the opportunity to explore and have fun learning about science. Now I actually like it." I have helped someone discover that science isn't just something that crazy guys in white lab coats do.

When I look around at the girls in my school, I wonder which girls spent a lot of time with Barbie growing up. Maybe they're the ones more concerned with what they look like on the outside and not on the inside. The ones who worry more about who will take them to prom than whether they will graduate from high school. The ones who worry about dating the guy who drives the newest model of car, when right down the street young kids are worrying about where they'll get their next meal. Don't get me wrong; I am not bitter, or even envious. I am proud of who I am. I am proud to be the girl who always wears those not very attractive sandals. I am proud to try to be that invincible revolutionary girl who wears her Birks.

Why This Essay Succeeded

From the first, stark sentence, Elisa draws us in with her rejection of Barbie—that all-American childhood toy. This essay would have fallen flat if Elisa did not do a sound job of showing why Barbie holds no interest for her and how her passions represent the exact opposite of what Barbie is perceived to be. Elisa's essay is very thoughtful without being overly philosophical. The part about dissecting Barbie to find her "empty" is a perfect image that captures how her intellectual curiosity contrasts to Barbie.

In her essay Elisa does not just tell us what she is not. She also provides an image of what she is: a pair of well-worn Birkenstocks. We see how the Birkenstocks came to symbolize perseverance and how she has learned to think on a large scale and be willing to contribute.

Throughout the essay Elisa incorporates her accomplishments without giving unnecessary detail. If the admission officers want to learn more about her work with the homeless or science fair achievements they can look at her application form. It would be a waste of space to reiterate what can be found elsewhere in the application. This is a prime example of when less is better.

Gabriel D. Carroll

Oakland, California

In the eighth grade, Gabriel wanted a way to take notes more quickly. He developed his own shorthand, Gastropodese, now a collection of more than 250 symbols that he still uses. This was just one indication of Gabriel's creativeness. As he applied to colleges, he wrote about solving math problems in Jack London Square, the importance of paper and his desire to become a cheese aficionado. His creativity is perhaps one of the reasons that he is incredibly gifted in mathematics. A graduate of Oakland Technical High School, he earned awards from competitions including the American Regions Math League and International Math Olympiad and won third place in the national Intel Science Talent Search for his project, "Homology of Narrow Posets." He wrote this essay to gain admission to Cornell but chose to attend Harvard University.

The Slice of Life
Cornell University

For years I have harbored a secret desire to become a cheese aficionado. This is not entirely arbitrary. Cheese, as an independent entity outside of any broader alimentary context, is at once worldly and whimsical. It provides the ideal complement to that side of my personality that has historically been dominant. My experiences have been largely rooted in the world of the abstract and the intellectual. Mathematics, music, writing and the like have given me a certain sense of detachment from reality. While I have historically enjoyed this detachment, there is always a desire to diversify. Eating cheese is a direct immersion in the world of the senses, where things are taken at face value. You don't analyze cheese, you just eat it—a refreshingly simple outlook on life.

At the same time, cheese offers the opportunity to express my individuality. There are plenty of more popular ways to get in touch with the earth, from cleaning to gardening to fishing, but I eschew the familiar. Cheese means uniqueness, or some approximation thereof. It also means independent imagination. Why be always bound to accepted notions of what is useful, what is interesting, what is respected? To take—for purely recreational purposes—something normally perceived as just one component of the kitchen and to turn it into a paradigm of its own requires both will and creativity.

And there is precedent: I like cheese. There are few sources of greater immediate gratification than munching a mozzarella, swallowing a Swiss or consuming a Camembert. My first encounter with a Parmesan—a solid block, not the Kraft grated stuff—was a revelation. Still, these are all among the more ordinary and pedestrian types of cheese. I feel a certain guilt in ignorance: I enjoy cheese, yet I have never gone beyond the average supermarket shelf to discover what infinitely more exciting flavors this world might hold. I have dreamed of remedying this discontentment, of ambling over to the local Barnes & Noble and finding a guidebook on cheeses and then of procuring samples of each, one by one, until I had developed a genuine familiarity with the world of cheese. Thus far, time and expense have seemed prohibitive. But there are always more opportunities.

Only after beginning the application process did it occur to me that Cornell is a highly appropriate place to pursue an interest in cheese. It would be logically connected to the existing dairy tradition. I don't know what food-oriented student organizations exist to back up my interest, but what with the famous wine-tasting course (to say nothing of the food programs at the college of Agriculture and Life Sciences), the university has at least a vaguely relevant academic tradition established. A large and diverse place, such as Cornell University, would be the most receptive setting for such an esoteric hobby.

The benefits of making cheese an acknowledged and regular part of my existence are essentially twofold. On one hand, it would mean realizing and developing a passion that has long been latent. On the other hand, it would be an integration of a new element into my personality, one that would simultaneously contrast with the existing elements and embody the same spirit of creative distinctiveness that I endeavor to infuse in the rest of my life. I define myself by what I do. I imagine being asked at parties: "What do you do?" "I am a mathematician," I would reply, including suitable detail. If pressed for more, "I also compose music, write poetry, code software, solve cryptic crosswords and play a mean game of Anagrams." After pausing an instant, I would add, "And I eat cheese."

Why This Essay Succeeded

Gabriel's essay is proof that virtually any topic can make a successful essay. He takes an everyday item (a food derived from mold no less!) and gives it meaning. Gabriel convincingly explains why cheese is significant to him and what it represents. While the essay is superficially about cheese, the reader really learns more about him.

There is an honest quality to Gabriel's essay. He does not try to present his interest as something more than it is. He does not pass himself off as a connoisseur with a vast knowledge of exotic cheese. He is just an amateur who truly enjoys eating cheese—something we can all relate to.

At the end of his essay, Gabriel includes a connection between Cornell and its academic programs and his love for cheese. While not essential, showing why a university is a strong fit to you is a good idea as long as it is appropriate for your topic.

Evan A. Coughenour

Bryn Mawr, Pennsylvania
Evan wrote his essay about something in which he believes—nine rules for being human given to him by his eighth-grade adviser. He says, "I was inspired by what I believe in and hold dear to me. The only way to write anything is to choose something that you really care about." At the Episcopal Academy, Evan was involved in lacrosse and music composition and performance. He plans a career in law.

The Rules for Being Human
Yale University

I question the process in which I go through life because I realize that I constantly fall short of my best. I see my life as a series of forks in a road, choices I must make to determine my path, decisions capable of leading me to a plethora of destinations. Whenever I begin to doubt my current path, I simplify the situation, asking myself not only where I want to go, but also more importantly "Are you enjoying each step that you take?" I want to squeeze the life out of each moment; I wish to value each day and live with meaning. Carpare diem volo.

My eighth-grade adviser gave me a simple document that encouraged me in this walk time and time again. I have read over all nine of "The Rules for Being Human" countless times as I lay in my bed, about to drift off to sleep, envisioning the places my path might lead. These rules apply in every situation, regardless of how frustrated, rested or experienced I may be. I walk a straight path only by accepting these rules and humbly allowing them to govern my aspirations.

Rule No. 2: "You will learn lessons." Mark Twain once said, "I have never let my schooling interfere with my education." Though I walk through the doors of The Episcopal Academy five days a week, I learn my most precious lessons not in these classrooms but in the classroom of life, with experience as my professor. I have never been "ready" to learn a lesson. The situations best suited for teaching take me out of my comfort zone and put a fork in my road; they require me to make a decision rather than allowing me to grow complacent.

I spent two weeks in July this summer in London, living with a host I did not know, in a town I had never before seen. Yet as I boarded my plane at the end of the trip bound for Philadelphia, I felt as if I was leaving my home, instead of returning to it. I woke up each day in London unsure of what I would learn, but reentered my flat at night amazed at the lessons laid out for me. I learned not to eat an Indian Kebab without a large water supply at hand to soothe my palate. I learned to look right before crossing the street, so that I might not meet an untimely end in London's inverted traffic patterns. On a more meaningful level, I found true happiness by putting aside my desires in order to love and serve those around me.

While in London, I concentrated on each individual experience, seeking to take something of value away from every moment. At home, however, I often cannot find such edifying episodes. Whenever I encounter this roadblock, however, I read Rule 3 and remember that all of my decisions can teach me if I remain open-minded about my daily experiences.

Rule No. 3: "There are no mistakes, only lessons." Dan Webster, now president of Authentic Leadership Incorporated, helped to firmly establish the value of making bad decisions in my mind. In choosing the wrong path, I unwittingly take the first step down the road to knowledge. Before starting down this road, however, I must choose to limit the damage I have done by confronting the consequences of my decision, putting away my pride and changing direction yet again. Rather than growing angry at this point, I look for the lesson hidden in my blunder and commit it to memory. Finally, I let go of this particular debacle, retaining solely the lesson I have learned. As Vivian Fuchs once said, "Good judgment is the outcome of experience—and experience is the outcome of bad judgment."

Rule No. 4: "A lesson is repeated until it is learned." I often find myself so fully consumed by life's paltry details that I have little time to reflect on a picture of greater importance. When I step back to look at my progress, I find that I have somehow been spinning my wheels, doing much but learning little. Almost a year ago, I wrote my first journal entry in response to this dilemma; I cannot believe that I ever could live in ignorance of such a valuable process. Writing each night on the unlined pages of my crimson book, I'm able to later use daily experiences as valuable teaching aides. When I take the time to read over past entries, lessons that I have never before recognized often become clear to me. When I read back in my journal, I search not for days in which all the facets of my life seemed to flow together smoothly, but for the times when thoughts and events have been the most misconstrued. As I relive these wrong turns, I learn to avoid repeating similar blunders.

Rule No. 5: "Learning lessons does not end." Every event in my life presents me with new lessons, yet I often pass them by, taking no notice of their value. A few years ago, a senior urged Episcopal's Upper School students to ask ourselves why we get out of bed each morning and automatically go to school or work. The more I thought, the more intrigued and philosophical I became. Of course, I got up in the morning because it was what I did every morning, but this answer left me unsatisfied. Did I go to school each day out of respect for my parents? What made me keep going? Why do I put up with these seemingly meaningless tasks? What was there to gain? As I pondered these questions though, my gaze wandered over to my bedstead, and I read over the quote which precedes this paragraph. Thus I awake each morning eager to seize a fresh day, for I always know that another lesson awaits me.

Why This Essay Succeeded

A lot of students get stuck when asked to explain their "life philosophy" or "beliefs." Evan avoids getting bogged down by choosing to share just a few of his rules for life. An essay doesn't need to give the whole pie; just a slice will do.

Evan also avoids the common mistake of parroting back someone else's words or thoughts. While he does share a few of "The Rules for Being Human," he uses examples from his life of how he has observed each rule. These concrete examples not only illustrate the impact of the rules but also help to keep the essay from becoming too much about the "rules" and not enough about Evan.

Notice that Evan is very deliberate in the examples that he chooses. His trip to London could have filled an essay all by itself. But by exercising restraint, which was probably not easy, Evan distills his London experience to a single paragraph that advances the overall theme of his essay.

Shor Bowman

Elk Garden, Virginia

Shor was sitting in his family's living room when he decided what he would write about for his application essay. He remembered back to a time when the room was a different color, the furniture was in the style of the 1970s and he transformed it into his personal art gallery. That became the topic he would write about. While at Lebanon High School, he participated in mock trial, forensics and singing in the choir. He wrote this essay for William & Mary but chose to attend the University of Pennsylvania.

The Bowman Gallery
William & Mary College

The artist squinted his eyes and observed the work that had just taken shape before him. The colors were vibrant, seemingly glowing independently of the light in the room. The detail was exquisite. The woman's arms were just in the right position to be playing the flute; the tiger seemed alive. Perfection had been achieved.

Detaching the work from the makeshift easel, he proceeded to change the page in the art book. "Hmm...what's this?" he asked himself. "Max Ernst's Oedipus Rex? Fabulous! I wonder if I have enough brown magic marker..." Placing another piece of white typing paper on the easel, he began to emulate yet another artistic masterwork to be hung proudly in the Bowmanden.

Art has always fascinated me and always been important in my life. From the day that I first discovered my mother's 2,000-page college art books, the colors, images and worlds depicted on canvas have held special meaning for me. Henri Rousseau, Henri Matisse, Franz Marc, Marc Chagall—they all did and still do captivate my imagination.

However, as a child in kindergarten, I was unable to find many people that shared my interest in painting. Many of my friends would rather have watched Michelangelo and Leonardo beat up Foot Clan members instead of looked at their murals and sculptures. I decided that I had to do something to change this Philistine viewpoint. Perhaps they just needed exposure! A trip to the Louvre was out of the question, but a trip to the Bowman household was not.

Thus, I began working tirelessly at reproducing the marvelous paintings that I found in the books. Armed with Crayola markers, ballpoint pens and an easel I made, I reproduced the works of such artists as Pablo Picasso, Paul Klee, Vincent Van Gogh, Georgio DeChirico and Claude Monet. I didn't view the task as labor, but I cherished it as entertainment and fulfillment. I loved reproducing such great works and being able to see how well my artistic talents were developing. When the dust had settled, I had reproduced 24 paintings in all. Considering the fact that an art display needed a gallery, I chose the Bowman family den as the location for the display. With the use of some scotch tape, the television room was transformed into a cultural mainstream, featuring works of the world's finest artists. My friends, unfortunately, never came. However, visitors that my parents had were treated to the art gallery and allowed to see and experience culture (or at least its carbon copy) firsthand.

As time for the Super Bowl came near, however, the gallery met with an unfortunate termination. Those drawings still exist and are definitely not forgotten. They serve as a testament to my ability and desire to create. They help to remind me that art is beautiful, that apathy will not do and that sometimes, enriching an intellectual environment requires that you get involved—sometimes to the extreme—and I will always be involved.

Why This Essay Succeeded

Through this essay Shor demonstrates he's not afraid to be different and daring. At an early age, he was exposed to—and more importantly—interested in famous artists. While his friends watched TV, he created reproductions of famous artwork. Shor shares the roots of his desire to learn and explore that he clearly carries onto later in his life. By taking us inside of his head we see what he saw when creating his masterpiece copies.

When writing about abilities, you don't always have to describe your current achievements, which may be detailed in other essays or parts of the application anyway. You can, as Shor has, show the admission officers a window into your heart, the genesis of your passion.

Stephanie Moy

Whitestone, New York

The first time Stephanie visited the Cornell campus she knew that it was her dream school. It didn't matter that she was 4 years old at the time. She gained the inspiration for writing this essay after speaking with her father, whom she describes as "rather philosophical." The two discussed how she had connections with both her ethnic culture and American culture. A graduate of Stuyvesant High School, Stephanie was co-captain of a technology event for the Science Olympiad and enjoys drawing the humanoid form and creative writing. She plans to work in web development or web design.

A Convergence of Clashing Beliefs
Cornell University

I grew up in a traditional Chinese family. All members of the older generations in my family are immigrants from China or the former British Colony of Hong Kong and still hold with them the customs and traditions they practiced in their homeland. Immersed in this sea of traditionalists I grew up thinking that American and Chinese cultures were identical. However my understanding has changed greatly since; although I still see both cultures as "identical," it is from a different perspective.

It wasn't until I began school that I became slightly exposed to American culture. Since I was young, my parents were protective of me and only occasionally allowed me to play with friends at their houses, thus decreasing my association with American families. When I began "American School," my parents also enrolled me in a Chinese School that met once a week. To me, Chinese School was simply an extension of the customs I already practiced at home. As a result, even if I had more interaction with non-Asian friends, my greater familiarity with Chinese culture gave me the impression that the customs of my ethnic homeland were the customs most Americans followed.

As I became more familiar with American culture, however, I began to fuse characteristics of and customs from both cultures and inherited a hybrid culture. For example, Chinese philosophy teaches us to maintain a low profile, that is, to not unnecessarily flaunt possessions and knowledge. Know your limit; never underestimate yourself, but do not push beyond your own abilities. American philosophy, on the other hand, encourages aggression and competition and acceptances of challenges, even those that may be too much to handle. There is an obvious clash in the beliefs of both cultures. While Chinese culture may be too conservative and wary, American culture likewise seems too aggressive and does not have enough caution against things not working out as planned.

Although the philosophies of either culture by itself may be too self-destructive or self-denying, I've found that it is efficient to pick the best from each and combine them to the best advantage for myself. For example, don't be too passive as Chinese philosophy advises, yet don't jump at every chance for promotion or raise as American philosophy suggests and possibly blow a blood vessel in the process. Rather, I find it most efficient to take the middle road, try new things and accept challenges with an open mind. Nevertheless, once your duties become too much to handle drop some less-significant activities and see how things work out. Instead of being an unknown entity or an arrogant big shot who announces every accomplishment in your life (and who will undoubtedly gain a few more envious enemies), make yourself known, but just enough so that people know who you are but not to the point that you are just another celebrity. This adaptation of two very different cultures converging is the "hybrid culture" that I follow.

Why This Essay Succeeded

Writing about culture (especially if you were raised in an immigrant family) is very popular. Unfortunately, most essays try to include every similarity and difference and in the end all sound the same. Stephanie is able to avoid this trap by focusing on just one major conflict between her two cultures: the Chinese tendency to show restraint versus the American tendency to be competitive.

She goes a step further by discussing how she has resolved this conflict. We can see from Stephanie's essay how taking the middle ground helped her to assimilate the two contrasting impulses.

When writing about a big issue such as the clash of cultures it is much better to do as Stephanie did. She broke down the topic into manageable parts and focused on just one or two aspects. This will almost always result in a stronger essay. Not to mention it will make your job of writing easier, too.

Mark R. Eadie
Rensselaer, New York

Mark was born with a desire to build, whether it was with his older brother's Legos or with hammer and nails. He has worked with his family to handcraft their own summer home and with his college classmates to build a national championship-winning solar car. At Columbia High School, Mark was an Eagle Scout, leader in his church and involved in Boys State and Model Congress. Through his essay, he says he wanted to give "an honest look at my life, what I've done and what I've had to deal with to do these things."

Building
University of Michigan

The week before my second birthday was my introduction to the world of Legos. My mother was busily getting ready for Christmas and needed to keep me occupied so she let me play with my 12-year-old brother's Legos. Although she did not think I would be interested, I sat on the carpet creating airplanes, cars and rocket ships for nine hours. That was the beginning of my love affair with engineering, design and building.

Soon clocks, motors, even new bicycles were not safe from my screwdriver or pliers, much to the consternation of my mother. My dad, a builder by avocation, was thrilled when I asked to help him and demanded an explanation of how everything worked as we repaired the house and added on to our summer camp. My father taught me many skills, how to build walls, plumb a bathroom, wire a house, lay hardwood floors, install windows and add cedar siding. Using many power tools and saws was fun, but the care I learned in planning and executing each step for highest quality was especially important.

In addition, I have an insatiable hunger for knowledge. When young, I read the *World Book Encyclopedia* and *Encyclopedia Britannica* as other kids read comic books and the backs of cereal boxes. No matter how much I learned I sought to know more. I wanted to understand the way things work more than I wanted the newest Teenage Mutant Ninja Turtle action figure. For my ninth birthday, my grandmother gave me a subscription to *Discover* magazine. I read every issue cover-to-cover, reading past bedtime to learn about fly-wheel engines, archaeological digs in China and the moons of Jupiter. I can never thank my "Grandmommy" enough for adding fuel to my fire for learning.

My father's and my latest project, due to our shared love of astronomy, was building a five-foot-long, six-inch diameter reflecting telescope with a Dobsonian mount. It was here I first really appreciated my dad's demand for perfection. After days of work, the result was incredible. The starry view is breathtaking—it adds so much to my excitement as I read Steven Hawking's and others' views on cosmology.

As the Senior Patrol Leader in my Boy Scout Troop, I have experienced the importance of teaching and inspiring younger scouts so they will develop the skills and values that I have learned. As an Eagle Scout, I had to design, organize and direct the troop in completing a major project. Utilizing the knowledge gained through working with my father and the communication skills developed through leadership in Boy Scouting and Presbyterian youth work, we extended the hiking trail system in our community by building a 20-foot by 4-foot bridge across a stream near the Hudson River. Not only is there satisfaction in seeing the completed bridge, there is the more important realization that my leadership is helping younger scouts develop into responsible, community-involved citizens. I'm very proud of them.

My church leadership role, as moderator of the Presbyterian Youth Connection Council for eight states, has allowed me to share my hope for the future, faith and vision with thousands in my generation and with adults across the Northeast.

Because of a baseball accident at age 10, the nerve in my right ear is dead, leaving me with only monaural hearing. Surgery did not work, and conventional hearing aids can't help people who are totally deaf in one ear. Fortunately, creative innovation combined with technological development has provided a "cutting edge" solution. A doctor in Connecticut has developed a trans-cranial hearing aid—the sound produced by the aid is transmitted so powerfully that it is conducted through the skull to the nerves in the good ear, on the opposite side of my head. With this, I can hear stereophonically as my brain interprets the second set of sound as though it was coming through my right ear.

As the beneficiary of one man's creative skills, I know what engineering can accomplish. The ability to examine a problem like unilateral hearing loss, create a new vision and solve the problem for people is the inspiration for my applying to Michigan's Engineering School. My faith and commitment to serve people motivates this drive. I want to use my insatiable desire to learn and create in order to advance technology for the benefit of others. The field of engineering is leading our society into more exciting developments than ever before, and I seek to use my leadership skills within this arena.

My vision is that aerospace engineering will allow humans not only to exceed the physical boundaries of our planet's limits but to grow intellectually beyond the constraints of terrestrial experience. In addition to all the practical earthly benefits that come from aerospace engineering, like biomedical, mechanical and materials breakthroughs, the philosophical and emotional benefits to humankind are extremely significant.

I want to attend the University of Michigan for love of engineering, for the challenge of it and to prepare myself to make a greater contribution to our society.

Why This Essay Succeeded

Mark's essay primarily shows the college how he became interested in engineering and why he is applying to the school of engineering. His descriptions of working with his father portray his insatiable appetite for learning how things work. It is clear that Mark wants to be an engineer not to make lots of money or because his parents are forcing him into it, but because he truly loves to build (and take apart) machines. Mark also alludes to a more personal reason for his desire to become an engineer. As the beneficiary of one engineer's invention, he regained his hearing.

While this essay covers a lot of ground, there is no doubt in the reader's mind why Mark will be a successful engineer. Notice, too, that Mark says nothing about his grades or academic courses—those are all self-evident in his transcript and test scores. By focusing on the "why" of his love for engineering, Mark makes his essay both original and memorable.

Elisa Lam

New York, New York

Elisa chose to write about a serious topic and demonstrate what she learned about herself and her family from the experience. Even though it was a trying situation, she explains how she grew closer to her mother from it. A second-generation Chinese American, Elisa is a first-generation college student and a graduate of Stuyvesant High School.

Growing Up
Cornell University

I was only 14 years old when I faced the realization that neither I nor the people around me were invincible. When I was young, I had always thought that my parents were like superheroes. They were always happy and had the answers for everything. Everyone knew that bad things didn't happen to good people, therefore my parents could not be hurt. This theory of mine was also applied to everyone else I knew. With this naive thought, I felt safe for many years even though I watched the news on television every day and listened to reports on tragic accidents and crimes. The news seemed to be contrived just for entertainment purposes. How could so many murders be committed by ordinary-looking people? How could there be so many stories about death and scandals? I dismissed these stories because I never thought I could be affected by them, they seemed to be so far away from me. Then one day I saw my mother cry.

Two months prior to this event, my family had spent the summer in Connecticut. My mother's first friend in America, Ann, had opened up a new business in a small suburban town and wanted us to come help out. Every day my father, mother, sister and I helped. Our family stayed over at Ann's new house the entire summer. In time, Ann and her husband became an extended part of our family. We spent every day together during times of work and play. I recall the fishing trips we had, the lazy days spent by the lake among wildflowers and dragonflies. I learned how to skip rocks and hook a worm that summer. By the time we had to leave, I had collected many happy memories and experiences.

Two months later, the entire family was sitting at the dinner table when I heard my mother gasp and put the newspaper down. This caught my interest and I scanned the page over her shoulder, not knowing what I looking for. Then I found it, a very familiar name—Ann's. There were no pictures; just an article in black and white. I had to read the story twice before I understood what it was saying. A woman had been shot twice in the head by her husband. After seeing what he had done, the husband shot himself. The bodies were discovered two days later. What was the motive for such an act? She had wanted to divorce him and marry someone else. I remember feeling dazed because I just couldn't believe that this could happen to two people I had spent so much time with. They had been happy and Ann's husband seemed nice and normal. I had spent every day of the past summer with this man, never doubting his sanity. I simply did not believe he was capable of such a deed. My mother was in shock. Five minutes later she was crying hysterically when she realized that her friend of over 15 years was really dead. I had never seen my mother cry before; she still rarely cries.

Though this experience was disturbing, it has given me a chance to get to know my mother better. My mother did not have relatives in America or many close friends, so she did not confide in many people. Being a traditional Chinese mother, she did not tell my sister and me much about what was going on or what she really felt. Because of this, my mother and I had never been particularly open about the everyday events in our lives. She was the mother and I was the daughter. She was to teach and I was to listen; this was our relationship. Ann was my mother's best friend, she knew almost everything about my mother's life. When she passed away, my mother had no one to talk to. I became my mother's confidant and friend. Over the past couple of years, we have shared secrets, hopes and dreams. Ann's death has also made me appreciate both my life and the lives of the people I care about more. The realization that things could change at any given time has definitely changed the way I see things.

Why This Essay Succeeded

Many students who write about a traumatic experience concentrate on describing the event. The successful essay must go beyond this, which Elisa has done exceptionally well.

By showing us how the death of her mother's friend affected her, Elisa allows us to learn more about who she is and how she deals with tragedy. Whenever you write about a specific experience—whether as dramatic as this one or not—think about how you can delve into the event beyond the standard "who," "what," "when," "where" and "why." A good essay needs to also answer the question of "how" such an experience affected or changed you or "how" you perceived the experience beyond the simple facts of the event.

Memorable Essay: Snow Junkie

Director of admission at Harvey Mudd College and former associate dean of admission at Pomona College

Do you feel that your life is boring? Sure you live in the suburbs and nothing exciting ever happens in the 'burbs. What could you possibly write about that is even remotely exciting?

Lots, says Peter Osgood director of admission at Harvey Mudd College and former associate dean of admission at Pomona College. In fact, Osgood keeps a personal file of all of the outstanding essays that he has read over the years.

He says one of the best essays in his file was written by a student from a typical suburban background. One of the student's school requirements was public service. Osgood says, "He wrote about how he was working with some inner city kids and they were taking a break to frolic in the snow. One of the kids made what looked like a snow angel. 'Hey, nice snow angel,' the student naively said. 'No,' the kid replied, 'I'm a junkie sleeping in the snow.'"

Osgood describes how the essay went on to explain how this incident hit the writer "right between the eyes" and made him think not only about what these at-risk kids see every day but also how such experiences can have a powerful cumulative effect. Osgood found the essay to be very thoughtful and appreciated that the student was able to recognize his sheltered upbringing.

You don't need to have had a life or death experience to write a great essay. If you spend time examining your life, you will discover something that is meaningful and that will make a successful essay.

Influential Books

Zane Curtis-Olsen

Charlotte, North Carolina

Zane has conducted research on nanotechnology and developed a method for measuring the electrical conductivity of retinal proteins. His research helped him become a member of the *USA Today* All-USA High School Academic Team and win a full scholarship as an Angier B. Duke Scholar. Through his essay he demonstrates that he can write about more than lab experiments. He delves into his personal influences. Outside of the classroom at Myers Park High School, he was the co-captain of his cross country team, state Hi-Q team champion and debate team captain. Offered admission to many selective colleges, Zane chose Duke University.

Santiago's Fight
Duke University

I've always been fascinated by far-off places and new and strange ideas. And that's affected my taste in books, a mix of ancient and medieval history, Japanese and South American literature, exotic philosophy and science books about the latest advancements in quantum physics and nanotechnology.

Yet, despite this, the book that has had the most profound affect on me is the definition of humble, and it took me no further than a small fishing village in Cuba. This was a book I read for school, *The Old Man and the Sea*, by Ernest Hemingway. At first, I didn't find it particularly special, a small book about a simple fisherman. Even when we learned about it in class, the message about humility and hard work sort of went in one ear and out the other. But then, our teacher gave us an assignment based on quotes we were supposed to find in the book. To find these quotes, I read the book about three or four times, looking for some of Hemingway's more poignant passages. It was in this search that I found this work a rather profound statement on humanity, the natural order of the universe and the eternal power of the human spirit.

Within Santiago's story, I found many of the themes I found in philosophy. Santiago has succeeded where so many existentialist philosophers have failed in finding his perfect place in our universe, and in doing so, Santiago has developed an understanding of the natural world equal to Lau Tzu's.

Santiago is a fisherman. Everything he does, he does to be a better fisherman, and in the end the desire to be the best fisherman leads him further than he has ever been before. And though he is a fisherman, he views the fish he catches and even the sharks that attack his caught fish as noble creatures who are as meant to swim and eat as he is to fish.

This sort of respect is something I feel a lot of people can learn from, including myself. Just imagine if our politicians had the sort of respect for their opponents that Santiago does. And I feel the idea of recognizing who you are and what you are meant to do and working to match that ideal can apply as much to any career as fishing. That the great Santiago is just a poor old fisherman also taught me about the dignity resting in every class and every profession.

Santiago's quest for his fish also says a lot about human nature. The statement can best be summed up in Hemingway's own words: "But man is not made for defeat. A man can be destroyed but not defeated." Santiago goes out on the sea for days and holds onto the giant marlin though it is constantly pulling against him and though one of his hands cramps. Once he has caught the fish, Santiago fends off sharks with every tool available to him. He knows the challenges presented to him are not impossible and does whatever he can to overcome them. I find this will to fight and succeed is an amazing human property and one that we can all take advantage of.

Why This Essay Succeeded

When colleges ask about a favorite book, they don't want a book report. What admission officers are looking for is your interpretation of the book and how it relates to you. Zane does this well in his essay. He draws connections between the book's major themes and his own views of life. From his essay, the colleges learn that he values respect of an opponent and taking pride in what you do.

When writing about an influential book, don't try to summarize the story. In fact, it's not really important for the reader to know the plot of the story or all of the main characters. Follow Zane's example and pick only the important ideas within the book that affected you. Reveal something about yourself through the impact and effect that these ideas had on your own life.

Svati Singla

Svati says that she has never let society's perception of age stop her. This was one of the factors that led her to publish an abstract in the *American Journal of Hypertension* after years of research—at the age of 11. Throughout junior high and high school, she continued her research at East Carolina University on fetal alcohol syndrome and won accolades from the U.S. Navy and Army. A graduate of J.H. Rose High School, Svati won an extraordinary $1 million in scholarships including the Discover Card Gold Tribute Award, Benjamin N. Duke Leadership Scholarship, Boy Scouts of America National Scholarship and National Merit Scholarship. After graduating, she plans to attend medical school.

Carpe Diem
Duke University

As humans, we constantly search for a truer and deeper understanding of life's many mysteries. Often, valuable life lessons come to us in the form of a sudden revelation, which then leads to motivation or inspiration.

When reading Joseph Heller's *Catch-22*, I encountered a revelation about human life that has led me to a greater understanding of the complex world around me. In this novel, Heller tactfully brings each of his characters to life through detailed descriptions and humorous anecdotes. However, just as the reader begins to form a slight attachment with the character, that lifelike individual suddenly disappears—either through death or some other mystery. As this pattern of life and death is constantly repeated throughout the novel, Heller carries a very important message to his readers—a lesson about the extreme fragility of human life.

Only after reading this novel did I realize how every day is a priceless opportunity; I realized how each day of life is truly a gift from above—a gift that must be cherished and utilized to its fullest extent. I was struck by the precarious nature of human life and by the inevitable prospect of human mortality; however, this inevitable future has given me great motivation and inspiration. Indeed, while absorbing Heller's message, the ancient Roman adage "Carpe Diem" (seize the day) rang through my mind. Realizing the impermanence of my life has encouraged me to make a difference in the lives of others. For only through a profound influence will my actions live on forever.

Why This Essay Succeeded

Svati demonstrates that in a short amount of space (about 250 words), it's possible to write a meaningful essay about yourself. But to do so you can't retell the story of the book. In fact, we learn very little about *Catch-22*. But we do learn about Svati. We learn what she found so compelling about Heller's novel and what it taught her about life. One of the biggest mistakes that students make is not drawing connections between the book and themselves. By making this connection, the admission officers learn more about who you are and what's important to you.

You will also notice that Svati does not actually analyze the plot of the book as much as its structure in the way Heller introduces and then suddenly removes characters. She is analyzing the story between the lines and then drawing conclusions about what Heller was attempting to say. And she does all of this is just a few sentences! The rest of her essay focuses on how this recognition of Heller's message has had an impact on her.

Emily Heikamp

Metairie, Louisiana

When exploring colleges in high school, it took Emily and her mother 14 hours to drive from Metairie to the North Carolina campus of Duke University. But it was time well spent. After her visit, Emily fell in love with the college. This is one of the essays she wrote to gain admission to and earn a full-tuition scholarship from Duke. In all, the self-described "science nerd" earned over $250,000 in scholarships. A graduate of Archbishop Chapelle High School, she plans to earn an M.D.Ph.D. in immunology or oncology.

Lessons from Harry Potter
Duke University

Like millions of 8-year-olds around the world, I have delighted in the wonder of *Harry Potter and the Sorcerer's Stone*. Although I am not 8, and I do not dart around my house with a broomstick, bathrobe and magic wand, Harry Potter is my hero. He gives a refreshing outlook of a benevolent world in which happiness can be achieved, villains can be conquered and the means of success can be learned. His intuition, intelligence and magic powers allow him to view the world as no one else can. He notices things that others do not, such as a tiny wizard shop on Diagon Alley or the train platform "nine and three-quarters." He is an intuitive, intelligent orphan with a destiny to triumph over evil. While most adopt a cynical view of the world, Harry's positive character gives hope that good can prevail. He defends his friends against the school bully and even defeats the evil wizard Voldemort in his quest to steal the Sorcerer's Stone. Harry is able to accomplish these feats because he has faith in himself. Professor Dumbledore, the headmaster at Hogwarts Academy, provides Harry with the support and guidance he needs to become a self-confident wizard. When Harry was disappointed, Dumbledore encouraged him, saying, "It's our choices, Harry, that show who we really are, far more than our abilities."

Harry Potter and the Sorcerer's Stone challenged me to look for things that others cannot see, to have faith that good will prevail and to believe in myself. I have learned to notice things that others often overlook, such as a homeless person begging for food, or even a friend who looks depressed.

I have embraced an optimistic perspective of the world, and I believe that people are good at heart. Most of all, I have gained confidence in myself and my choices. I have learned to become secure with my insecurities, to be fair when justice is unpopular and to have courage in the face of adversity.

Why This Essay Succeeded

Who says a book has to be a classic to be influential? There is nothing wrong with selecting a book that has mass-market appeal. By choosing *Harry Potter and the Sorcerer's Stone*, Emily shows her less serious side. This is, after all, a children's book! But even though she selects a children's book, she does not write about it in a childish or immature way. In fact, she analyzes the characters in the same way she would had she chosen a classic read in English class. Emily also makes sure to relate Harry's life philosophy to her own. We see in her the same optimistic perspective on life and personal courage that Harry displays in the novel.

When selecting a book to write about, it's important to follow your heart. In other words, choose the book that truly speaks to you. If it's a children's book or comic book, so be it. As you can see from Emily's essay, it doesn't really matter if the book is from your senior English class or your childhood. What counts is how inspired you are to write about it.

Jonathan S. Gnoza

Staten Island, New York

It seems that Jonathan could have lived in another time, even another century. He is impassioned by Arthurian legend, the geometry of Euclid and the astronomy of Ptolemy. Likewise, he won the New York Classical Club Latin Sight-Translation Contest three times, placed Summa Cum Laude in the National Latin Exam three times and tutored peers in Latin. A graduate of Regis High School, he plans to become a professor in the classics.

Arthuriana
Harvard University

On a certain day I was eating lunch with my friends Tom and Peter, and we were discussing which of our classmates were characters; that is, people who distinguished themselves with a unique and often slightly eccentric trait. At one point Tom turned to me and told me that I was not a character. I intended to object, but Peter voiced his disagreement first, responding that my incorporation of ancient and medieval values into my modern life indeed defined me and qualified me as a character. I was rather pleased by this recognition of my personality.

This defining preference for things which predate the Prostestant Reformation derives from the reactions which I experienced while reading some selections from Sir Thomas Malory's *Le Morte D'Arthur*. I enjoyed it so much that I soon decided to read a complete version. The search for an unabridged edition took me to a few different libraries and stores, and at last I borrowed one from my grandparents' library. Based on my enjoyment of the short version, I expected that I would like the full version even more. Indeed, from the point when I opened the first page of that book, I was completely obsessed with it. I read it everywhere; during the summer, I finished the whole book twice, and over the past four years, I have reread my favorite parts countless times. The primary reason why I read it so much was for the pleasure, but subconsciously I think I was reading it to imitate it.

Immediately, the book drove me to learn more about Arthurian legend, history and literature. Arthuriana became a hobby that I pursued with intense zeal. I bought and read many books on the topic, sometimes going to tremendous lengths to find them; I made special orders from bookstores, spent hours in the big research library in Manhattan and searched for online dealers of used books since many of the titles I wanted to read were out-of-print.

Malory's book also inspired my curiosity toward medieval culture in general, especially its moral ideals. I have found certain qualities of the code of chivalry to be universally admirable: trust, loyalty, truth, honor and helping people in need. I have tried to instill them in my own character with practices such as not cheating, avoiding falsehoods and tutoring other students. Many a one would let another have one's seat on the subway, but I do so because I think to myself that is what a knight would do.

Like Sir Galahad, though, I also realize that holiness is important. The chapter about the Quest for the Holy Grail showed me the value of a more intimate relationship with God, especially through daily prayer and acceptance of His will. Reflecting on this now, I see that this change had more meaning than just a desire to be prepared in case the Holy Grail should miraculously return to earth. In the example of those who found the Grail, I discovered what I had been seeking: a real culmination for all the learning I received in Catholic school. The book was my personal guide to a spirituality that I found lacking in my experiences with the modern world.

Captivated by such medieval interests, I jumped at the chance to take Latin at Regis, and it has been my favorite subject because it is a major key to unlocking the ideas of past ages. I have totally immersed myself in Latin, and further love my ancient Greek, which I started this year. Beyond classical grammar, though, I have undertaken the relearning of geometry from Euclid, music theory from Pythagoras and Aristoxenes and astronomy from Ptolemy. When everyone in my physics class had to do a book report on a work in that subject, everyone was reading Stephen Hawking, Albert Einstein or the like, but I read *Physics* by Aristotle. This gave me more pleasure and personal satisfaction than everything else I did for physics because it was an interdisciplinary experience linking science and classics.

In the school's chess club, where love for one of the oldest known games is typical, people have called me especially traditional on account of my preference for the classical openings. Similarly, I prefer the early medieval, Christian, Uncial style of calligraphy and in this script, I have copied the books of Habakkuk, Jonah and Zephaniah as they were written in St.

Jerom's Latin Vulgate. My hobby of archery, which I practice very informally, is yet another way in which I have defined myself as one who seeks to relive and revive ancient and medieval ways.

Why This Essay Succeeded

One of the questions admission officers ask themselves after reading an essay is, "Would I like to meet this student?" Some even ask, "Would I like to be this student's roommate?" After reading Jonathan's essay, the admission officers resoundingly said, "Yes!" Both in his style of writing and choice of topic, Jonathan creates such a unique portrait of himself that you can't help but want to learn more.

What makes his essay so powerful is that Jonathan is able to share so much about himself. In addition to describing his passion for his favorite book, he also uses the title to convey his personal philosophy, academic interests and extracurricular activities. This is a lot to include in an essay, but he does so seamlessly.

After reading Jonathan's essay, you may think that you must have a truly unique personality to make an impression on the admission officers. The truth is that you don't have to be interested in Arthuriana as Jonathan is. It's important to remember that even if you think of yourself as "normal," you have something interesting within you. The key is to figure out what that is and how to share it in your essay. When you are done writing your essay, have someone else read it and ask them: "If you were an admission officer would this essay, make you want to meet me?"

Essays About Family

Zane Curtis-Olsen

My Mother's Influence
Harvard University

I know it sounds like a cliché to say that the person who has had the most influence in my life is my mother, but there's a reason why things become clichés. It's because there's always a bit of truth to them.

I love my mother, of course, because she's my mother. She's always taken care of me, fed me, clothed me and been there when I needed her. But even if she weren't my mother I would still admire Mary Cecelia Curtis as a person and look at her as a role model.

She's worked hard and accomplished a lot, but this hasn't detracted from her commitment to family and friends. And she's never been satisfied with what she's accomplished. She's always trying to be a better person and develop professionally. For instance, she is a department head at a newspaper supervising a large staff and many sections. But in the last year, she took on the challenge of writing a weekly column. She also helps with recruiting at her newspaper because she is committed to bringing more African-Americans to the staff.

Her path has not been easy. She was one of five children in a working class family in Maryland, and despite the obstacles and the subtle (and sometimes not so subtle) racism she faced, she persevered. She graduated Summa Cum Laude from college and slowly worked her way up as a journalist, eventually becoming a respected section editor at the *New York Times*.

She has always served as a mentor to other minority journalists and continued to teach young journalists in programs such as those offered by the Maynard Institute.

The success and influence my mother has had in the world of journalism provides a model for the success and influence I hope to have in the world of science. And, like my mother, I hope I can mesh personal and professional challenges. I also hope to help those who come after me. I know the path in science I've chosen is difficult, but after seeing all the hardships my mother has worked through, I'm ready for the challenge.

When I first arrived at the Research Science Institute program at MIT, I was a little daunted. I realized that of the 70 young math and science scholars from around the world I was the only African-American. I thought about my mom and realized that needn't be an obstacle and that I could make my way and distinguish myself in any setting.

Working with an associate professor of physics at UNCC in the field of Near Field Scanning Optical Microscopy, I found I had to learn a lot and persevere through much failure to succeed. It was lucky I could recall the quality of perseverance my mother has modeled for me.

I suppose any essay about my mom always comes back to the personal. She encourages me and loves me; she disciplines me and expects a lot, but she's always there—even when I fall short. There's only one problem. When I have children of my own, she will be a hard act to follow as a parent.

Why This Essay Succeeded:

Parents are a dangerous topic to write about if not done carefully. The odds are that thousands of other applicants will be writing about Mom and Dad. How do you make yours stand out? Zane demonstrates how you can write about a common topic in an uncommon way. The key is to be specific and not get bogged down in unimportant detail. Notice that Zane quickly summarizes the highlights of his mother's life that inspire him. He then turns the focus of his essay 180 degrees toward himself. As much as we learn about his mother, we also learn about Zane.

Ultimately, who the admission officers really want to know about is you. While you will need to describe the person, don't forget that you must tie in their influence, values or lessons back to your life. After all, it's not Mom who is applying for admission but you!

Daniel Heras

Los Angeles, California

When you think of East Los Angeles, you probably don't think of surfing. But one student does. Daniel bucked convention to become one of the few in his community to take to the ocean, the topic of his essay. At Woodrow Wilson High School, he was student body president, captain of the baseball team and president of the science club. Daniel wrote this essay to counter critics who said that college would not be an option for him. "There was that one little voice that told me to keep trying and to never give up," he says.

Surf's Up! In East LA?
U.C. Berkeley

In my family everyone grows up playing soccer. It is not a question. You just do it. Although I played soccer, it was not the same for me. Dashing back and forth on a 120-yard field, kicking a ball around and not being able to use your hands was not my idea of living. It was not until about three years ago when I found myself slipping off a seven-foot-long piece of fiberglass and Styrofoam, landing head first into the deep blue sea when it slapped me right in the face. Surfing was for me! It was not just my image of living life, but living life on the edge.

Riding waves was not an easy thing to do, and I mean that in two ways. First, surfing is a difficult task, period. Just the laborious thought of being a surfer alone was inconceivable. I had never in my life seen a surfer except on TV. None of my friends surfed, and it was unheard of in East LA to see a Hispanic surfer. At first I never told anyone that I had been surfing. I kept it to myself, though it was very hard to hide a seven-foot-long board in my sock drawer. My friends would come over to my house and say, "What the heck is that?" Of course, I had to tell them even though I knew how they would react. They would just laugh and say, "You ain't no surfer, you're a wannabe." I would stay quiet. Some nights while lying in bed, I would think: Was this just a phase? Was I trying to be someone that I really was not? Was I really a "wannabe"?

At times failure would make me think that surfing would just be a small chapter in my life. I remembered the closing days of summer a few years ago. I got up early that morning to get ready for my short 20-minute trip to Venice Beach. Something seemed different that morning. I felt bold, I felt confident and I was immortal. (Not really.) The day was perfect. I did it, the first wave I saw and was up and in it. I cannot say I did not fall that day, because I did. But after eight long weeks of nothing but sand in my face, I was on top of the world. I persevered. It was not going to be just a phase.

No matter what race: Black, White, Asian, Hispanic or any other race, people living in East LA do not become surfers. But here at the Heras residence, you do find the rarity. I have discovered who I am. I am coura- geous, unique and at times I am not always going in the same direction as everyone around me. But this is alright. Sometimes reacting unlike anyone else leads to success. No one tells me I have to play soccer, I have to tag on walls or even own a lowrider bike. My family does not pressure me to get a job right out of high school or go to community college part time. Just because so many here do, that does not mean I have to do it too. Look- ing back, the decision to surf instead of play soccer has made me a more versatile person. It made me love life, it made me stop and think and be thankful for everything around me. I feel that if my decision to surf did this for me, then other decisions, like my decision to pursue the highest level of education, will be even better. This proves that being a little bit on one's unique side can sometimes be the best.

There was a time in my life when I did not know who I was but as a result of surfing I now know who I really am. I also know that surfing will not just be a small chapter in my life but the recurring theme that holds the story of my life together. I am not a "wannabe."

Why This Essay Succeeded

Daniel uses his interest in surfing as a clever analogy to introduce his willingness to do the unexpected. Through his essay we see that he has faced many people who questioned his ability to succeed personally and professionally. His essay takes us through his thought process to show us why he's become so motivated to overcome these naysayers and we can appreciate what he has accomplished.

As you're writing, it's important to always take this extra step of not just describing but explaining. Having this analysis or reflection is critical and makes the difference between a successful and unsuccessful essay. Remember, you want to impress the admission officers not only with your ability to write but also with your ability to think.

Daniel Saat

Rochester, New York

It was his father's unique approach to business and to life in general that influenced Daniel to write this essay about the duo's experience in an open-air market in Israel. Daniel may follow in his father's footsteps with his desire to work in marketing or consulting. At Brighton High School, he was the regional president of the Distributive Education Clubs of America. He was also an all-state saxophone player, varsity baseball player and active member of United Synagogue Youth. Daniel wrote this essay to gain admission to the Wharton School of Business at the University of Pennsylvania.

The Beer-Sheva Marketplace
University of Pennsylvania

We stroll through a marketplace in Beer-Sheva, inhaling a conglomeration of smells and sounds that feel as though they are part of a different century. My father and I enter a small stand. A little woman sits in the corner scanning her livelihood like a hawk monitoring her nest. She promotes her wares not for a quarterly report but to feed and clothe her family. My father picks up a small wooden camel and calls out in our native tongue, "How much?"

"Fifty shekel," she responds. Her reply is automatic. This is what she does all day, every day.

My father eyes her directly. He doesn't flinch. "I'll give you 10." He remembers the game as if he'd been playing it daily since he left his homeland. She opens high and he counters low, each one hoping the other will give in first. I observe, taking mental notes.

She replies with conviction, "It's handmade, I can't go lower than 40." We all know the camel was made in a local factory, but he doesn't contradict her. To call her credibility into question at this stage could ruin the transaction.

"I only have 20," fires my dad, as if he had rehearsed his line. I glance at his back pocket bulging with Israeli currency but don't let on, for she's searching my face for a sign of weakness. I'm beginning to see what the game is all about.

"I cannot sell for less than 40," she retorts. My father squeezes my hand subtly and I latch on to his paw. We slowly start to leave the stall.

"So be it," he voices over his shoulder with an air of studied ease. We continue out of the cool shadows toward the fascinating frenzy of the exotic streets.

Just as our sandaled feet touch the dirt road and we are about to rejoin the crowd, we hear a shriek. "Wait! Give me 30." My father winks at me, turns nonchalantly and swaggers toward the woman. I quickly pull 30 shekel out of my pocket and thrust them into his hand, so the woman won't discover the treasures buried in his pocket. I smile at my quick thinking. My father plays it straight, as if I were supposed to hand him the money.

He works his thick fingers around a 5-shekel piece and with a magician's sleight of hand swiftly transfers the coin to his other palm. "I only have 25." The woman hastily nods.

The negotiations are successful. The woman is satisfied for she had invested only 10 shekel in the knickknack. My father smiles. While he would have paid any price for the camel, he enjoyed the challenge of a worthy opponent. We rejoin the streets to once again immerse ourselves in those ancient sounds and smells.

From my earliest childhood, I have learned many such fascinating business concepts at my father's side. These experiences have long intrigued me. Formulas, figures, accounting cycles and textbooks do not tell the whole story. Cultural traditions of negotiation, respect and the dynamics of people coming together to buy and sell are the most captivating parts of trade. Society is an interdependent web, relying on its members to meet each other's needs. Business is centered on the exchange of one good or service for another in an effort to improve society's standard of living. The intricacies, methods and strategies involved in this exchange are what I hope to acquire and master.

Why This Essay Succeeded

Daniel's essay works because he not only shares his relationship with his father but also draws astute conclusions from his interaction. He takes the time to explain the meaning of the experience and uses it to give insight into his interest in business. Through his essay, you learn about him on a personal level through the way he relates to his father as well as on a professional level by seeing his career goals.

A successful essay is not just an interesting story. What captivates the admission officers is the meaning within the story. This is the real challenge of the essay.

Memorable Essay: Melodies Of Life
Director of Admissions, Lawrence University

There are some topics that are just plain hard to write about. Music is one of them. But if you can write well about something like music, it can be very impressive.

Michael Thorp, director of admissions at Lawrence University, has read many poor essays about music. Despite the fact that music is such a difficult topic, it was the subject of one of the best essays he recently read.

The student wrote about playing a Bach overture. Thorp says, "What made this essay truly special was that the student was able to reflect upon the music's effect on the people around her."

"She included a description of a student outside her normal peer group who was sitting next to her and how through the music they were playing they bridged the social chasm that existed. It was well-written. It was imaginative. It gave me a true glimpse into her personality. It was a brilliant essay," raves Thorp.

Don't be afraid to tackle a difficult topic. Often while more time-consuming to write, they can make extremely effective essays.

Robin Potts

Richmond, Virginia

When her father became ill, Robin realized for the first time that her parents weren't invincible. She says, "I thought they were perfect, but they have problems, too." Robin decided to write about her parents because she wanted to write about what meant the most to her. A graduate of Collegiate High School, she plays piano, was captain of the cross country team and member of the soccer and indoor track teams and participated in the Federal Reserve Challenge, presenting a project with her team to the Fed. She plans to work in the financial industry.

Twelve Bobby Pins
Harvard University

The middle-aged woman bending over my father seemed different that day. As she gently spoon-fed homemade chicken soup to her husband, years of worry and exhaustion revealed themselves under her swollen eyes, across her ridged forehead and in her hollow cheeks. Although she carried her head high as she doted over the weak man, her gray eyes betrayed her strong composure and showed her weaknesses, her sorrow and her fear. Her once fluorescent eyes now appeared faded as if drained by the passage of time.

Occasionally, I caught her sighing as she slowly brushed a few loose strands away from her face. The rest of her slightly over-colored hair was fastened by bobby pins into a tight twist. Like always, she had used more pins than were needed. I had often argued with her over this point, trying to prove to her that five pins rather than twelve would be more than sufficient to hold her hair in place. She had always responded good-naturedly and applauded my level-headed reasoning. However, she still insisted on using twelve pins. Watching her now dab my father's lips with a neatly pressed linen napkin, I realized that she had known well before our discussion that the use of twelve bobby pins was absurd. But, it was their very absurdity that saved her, protected her and guarded her from the unknown evils of the universe. Their clinging presence prevented her from becoming undone. They provided stability when life could not.

I had never before recognized these details of age in my mother. In place of wrinkles, I had seen lines of laughter. In place of graying hair, I had seen strands of vibrancy. And in place of absurdity, I had seen reason. During childhood, I had believed so heavily in her strength that I had never perceived her weaknesses. Now, as I surveyed the pale outstretched fingers that stroked my father's hairline, I understood another side of her. Like me, she had troubles, unanswered questions and fears. She, too, lay awake nights, restless with thoughts of how the future might unravel. Despite her wishes, she could not pin the future motionless like her hair. Challenges would arise whether she used twelve pins, five pins or no bobby pins at all. Perhaps it was this realization that had produced some of the deep lines above her eyebrows, beneath her eyes and around her lips. With these lines, she showed her comprehension of reality and exposed this understanding to the world.

As I studied my mother's affectionate motions, my eyes met hers. Without words, her expression told me that the fatigued man before us would survive. He might not recover from surgery today, tomorrow or even next week, but with her loving medicine, he would eventually pull through. I smiled at this reassurance and returned her warm gaze. And then, I saw her eyes twinkle. The clouded, gray eyes shed their foggy covering, releasing countless rays of grace. The gentle beams streamed out from within her soul to illuminate every inch of the room. Although this lucent sensation lasted but an instant, I will remember it for a lifetime. The spark, which had occurred as a result of her selflessness, awakened me to the true meaning of "strength." This word did not connote powers of invincibility as I had once envisioned, nor did it entail the suppression of all weaknesses. Instead, strength, as I had seen illuminated in my mother's eyes, implied the ability to be dignified under stress. I marveled at the realization that my mother possessed one of humanity's greatest qualities. This serene woman, though weak in appearance, exemplified more strength than I could imagine. Thus, as I stole one last glance into her eyes, or rather into her, I vowed that someday my eyes would also radiate such beams of power, compassion and courage.

Why This Essay Succeeded

Some students feel they must write about a lifetime's worth of experiences in their essay. Robin's is proof that the description of a single moment can be more than enough. Her essay shares so much about her mother and herself. While Robin writes about a very common topic (Moms and Dads), she does so in a way that no one else will. By focusing on a specific aspect that is unique to her, Robin guarantees that her essay will be original.

If you write about a person, you may not have as dramatic an experience to share as Robin. But what's important is not the drama but how you make the experience your own. Think about the person—whether a parent, relative or friend—and how you can share a unique perspective about him or her, and in so doing, about yourself.

Elisa Tatiana Juárez

Hurricane Andrew
Brown University

On one of the two walls of bookshelves in my new room, you will see a photo album. When you open this album, images of my past appear. You may notice that what makes my photo album different from most other teenagers' albums is that it starts when I was 8. Not because my parents didn't love me or take cute baby pictures of my broth

er and me, but because I was confronted at that age by a meteorological monster named Andrew. On August 23 our family really didn't think the storm would hit Miami, but we cleaned the entire house from top to bottom and did the other hurricane preparations. My mom's logic was that we might not have any electric power or water for awhile, so the house should be clean. We lived in a two-story house, so my brother and I set up a place to "camp" in a closet downstairs, just in case. At about midnight, the storm path had turned its course and headed directly toward us, so our parents moved us into the closet in their bedroom.

That night is still very vivid in my mind. I remember lying on a blanket on the floor of my parents' bedroom closet and being awakened by a very loud noise. I later learned that it was our backyard play fort that my dad had set in concrete, slamming against the side of the bedroom. I remember that my papá was holding a portable battery-powered radio and muttering things to himself, "vientos a 200 millas por hora...nos está pegando fuerte...el ojo de la tormenta casi llega...lo peor todavía falta" Yes, the worst was still to come. Until that moment, I had never felt so helpless. My house was blowing away around us, chunk by chunk; there was very little keeping my family and me from being swept away. Worse, there was nothing I could do, nothing anyone could do, but wait and pray. Suddenly there was silence. Complete and total silence. There was no noise, not even the chirp of a bird. My papito got up and ventured beyond the closet door. He forced the door open, only to realize that he was pushing against insulation and dry wall from the remains of our house. He said almost everything was gone, but everything was calm, there wasn't even a breeze in the air. I felt that I shouldn't even breathe, for fear of disrupting the silence. What was next? Who knows? We weren't prepared for any of this.

Suddenly out of nowhere, the silence was broken. The winds picked up again, and we braced ourselves for more. The next few hours can be played in my mind, like a movie. I can pause it whenever I want, zoom in and out and fast-forward past the most terrible moments. I clearly remember my father calling my mother to help him keep tornado-force winds from coming into the bedroom. The walls were cracking around us; water was pouring into the room. The air pressure dropped drastically within the house.

Then, as soon as it all started, it was quiet again. We didn't know what to do. Was it OK to wander out? Was it over, or was that just another false hope? My parents ventured out first. They came back and told us quite simply "Well, you know what? God gave us a beautiful sunroof." A sense of humor, I learned, is essential at a time like that. They made a path through the rubble to allow my brother and me to see what was left of our rooms. I walked out of the cubbyhole that had kept us safe for the past eight hours, and was not at all prepared for what came next. Mom was right when she said we had a sunroof, well if you can call it a sunroof. There was nothing. I looked up and saw the cloudy morning sky from what had been our living room. In the place where my room used to be, there was only a huge, empty cavity. The floor was pink and fluffy with building insulation materials. My great-grandmother's piano was totally covered in wet fiberglass and the remains of a popcorn ceiling. The family heirloom piano had just arrived at our house, a gift from my grandmother in Texas. It was destroyed. My dog that we had locked into the bathroom across the hall was whimpering in a corner. To this day, she is terrified of storms. I wanted to crawl into a corner myself, but although I was only 8 I felt I had to be strong. As a family we walked into the rooms, or what was left of them, to inspect what had happened.

I stood in the doorway, separating what were once the kitchen and the backyard. Looking out I saw the real damage. Houses were no more than piles of toothpicks. Looking around me, I shed my first and only tear. There was no time to cry. We all had to get stuff out of the house before the mildew set in.

We found our way to the main doorway and dared to walk outside to find out what the rest of the world looked like. The rest of the people in our neighborhood had the same idea. All of us were in total shock. Everyone looked at each other, standing in what was left of their doorways, and an unspoken understanding was communicated. Our next-door neighbor, a former Green Beret, assured us that "someone would be here to help us soon." Less-confident neighbors started to move trees from the middle of the street in order to clear a path, just in case help couldn't get to where we were.

The first night, we moved in with our cousins, who lived a few blocks down what used to be a street. Only part of their house had caved in, the bedrooms were damp, but livable. As I tried to fall asleep that night I realized that yes, I had lost everything that I had valued on a material level, but I still had what was most important, my life and my family. I could replace the things I had lost, even the piano, but my father's smile, my mother's protectiveness and my brother's sense of humor were all irreplaceable.

I survived; it was almost as if I had been given a second chance at life. At that early age, I realized that our family easily could have been killed. If we had been in a different room, if the hurricane had hit us at a different angle or if the tornado had entered the room, I wouldn't be here. Life is delicate and precious. I knew I couldn't live my life as a silent impartial observer; I had to do as much as I could and enjoy every day because we only have one life and only one chance to make a difference.

Why This Essay Succeeded

While not every student experiences a tragedy as traumatic as Elisa did, you can describe yourself through a difficulty that you've overcome. Elisa does an excellent job of relating not only what happened to her family during and after the hurricane but also what she gained from the natural disaster.

Throughout her essay, Elisa uses vivid, dramatic descriptions of specific moments to help us understand the experience of riding through a hurricane. But just as important, Elisa shows us how her parent's reactions—whether it's her father's calm composure or the joke about having a new sunroof—made this occurrence more than just an act of mother nature. Anyone can write about wind and rain. It's the storm or calm inside that counts in your essay.

Gen S. Tanabe

Waialua, Hawaii

One of the authors of this book, Gen turns an ordinary, everyday experience into a powerful essay. He wanted an essay that not only conveyed his accomplishments but that also relayed the special relationship that he had with his family and his father in particular. At Waialua High School, Gen was president of the student body, captain of the debate team and vice chairman of the Hawaii state student council.

Dad's Pancakes
Harvard University

In spite of the various extracurricular activities I've done and interesting people I've met, not one event or person has been more meaningful to me than my father's preparation of breakfast.

Every morning I wake up to the sounds of my father cooking breakfast. While lying in bed, I try to guess if the clank of a pan means scrambled eggs or maybe his specialty, banana pancakes. Waking up to nearly 7,000 such mornings, I have grown to admire my father's dedication, a dedication that never falters even after hours of late-night work.

I readily applied this value of dedication when I was elected Vice-Chairman of the State Student Council. With the tremendous amount of work related to this position, there were numerous occasions when I found myself having to choose between reviewing Board of Education policies and going to the beach with friends. And whenever I felt myself beginning to vacillate, I was always reminded of my father's unwavering dedication. I knew that the students who elected me depended on my dedication, and like my father's daily commitment, I would not let them down.

Whenever I hear my father making breakfast I always hope that he is preparing his piece dé résistance, banana pancakes. My father's pancakes are not generic "Bisquickies," but one-of-a-kind masterpieces. He uses scratch ingredients from hand-sifted flour to homegrown bananas. As I grew older I noticed that I also began to assume the same ambition toward life as my father has toward his pursuit of the perfect pancake.

In my freshman year I took an interest in film making and soon my goal was to own a video camera and recorder. To accomplish this goal I could either wait six months until Christmas and hope Santa could afford a new VCR, or I could earn the money and buy it myself. My ambitious yearning took over and for the next three months of summer vacation I held a brush in one hand and a can of latex in the other as the hired painter of my grandmother's house. Although the work was hard and tiring, by the end of the summer, I was able to earn the money to fulfill my goal. Having learned from my father to strive for success, I have since worked fervently but patiently to attain my goals in life.

After my father has flipped the last pancake, the best part of breakfast has arrived—consumption. As I devour the stack of scrumptious pancakes, I notice that my father has a bright smile across his face; I am not the only one to savor this moment. My father truly enjoys making my breakfast. My father's joy from even the simplest things has been the model that I have tried to apply to my life every single day.

Failure to heed my father's lesson was disastrous in my sophomore year when I decided it would be impressive to become a cross country runner. As I was running the three-mile course, I began to realize around the second mile that I did not particularly enjoy running. In fact I hated running. This painful experience reminded me of my father's overarching aim to enjoy what he is doing. Since then I have chosen to excel in tennis and other activities, not for the prestige or status, but simply because I enjoy them.

My father completes the tradition of preparing breakfast by soaking the dirty pans in the sink. As he does, I think of how fortunate I am. Some people only have one meaningful event in their lives, but I have one every single morning.

Why This Essay Succeeded

Since this is my (Gen's) essay I'd like to give you a behind-the-scenes look at how and why I wrote it.

To find an original idea is not always easy. I spent several days just listing topic possibilities. On my list I wrote my father's name since he was very influential. Under his name I outlined admirable qualities one of which was that he made me breakfast each morning. When I zeroed in on that aspect I realized how much care he put into my favorite–banana pancakes. Although I continued to brainstorm every time I looked at the list this one aspect–banana pancakes–kept drawing my attention.

That's when I began to write. I am not a naturally good writer. It takes me many, many re-writes to be able to express on paper what is in my mind. I probably wrote this essay more than a dozen times. Each time it got a little better and more focused. When I thought it was just about perfect I shared with two of my favorite English teachers.

When I got back their comments I thought a bottle of red ink had exploded. Most importantly, they had the perspective of a first time reader. I was so close to the story that I didn't realize there were sections that needed more explanation or transitions that weren't smooth. This feedback was critical and I went through an additional half dozen re-writes.

It took about a month from the time I started brainstorming to the day I had a finished essay in hand. It really helped to be able to let the essay ferment. There were days that I thought it was perfect, only to re-read it a day later and find all sorts of problems. The best advice I have for writing an admission essay is to give yourself the time you need to discover your own masterpiece.

Influential People

Jacqueline Ou

Lexington, Massachusetts

Jacqueline is thankful for her junior high math tutor. Mr. Chase helped her build the foundation for impressive achievements. In addition to the math honors she describes in her essay, she was a member of the *USA Today* All-USA Academic First Team, a Siemens Advanced Placement Scholar for being the highest scoring female junior in New England on the math and science AP exams and a semifinalist in the Intel Science Talent Search. At Lexington High School, Jacqueline led a student-directed a cappella group and a traditional Chinese dance troupe, edited for the newspaper and won first place in the state for her National History Day paper.

Polyhedra
Duke University

In the back of my dresser sits a set of old, beaten-up plastic polyhedra lying dusty and unused. I haven't touched them for years, since the time in sixth grade when I filled the pyramid, sphere and cone with dyed water to compare their volumes and spilled water all over the kitchen chairs. I spent forever cleaning the stains out of those white chairs! I had to stick my polyhedra into storage after that, because Mom banned me from ever mixing polyhedra, food dye and kitchen chairs again in my entire life, or at least while I was still living under her roof.

One afternoon a few weeks ago, soon after learning about the death of my friend and math tutor, Mr. Chase, I suddenly get an impulse to dig the polyhedra out of their hiding spot. I finger the cracked plastic container and lift the hexagonal prism, once my favorite polyhedron, out of the box. Holding the chipped prism in my hands, in a moment's time I am taken back to bits and pieces of the afternoons when Mr. Chase and I explored polyhedra together. The flashbacks of all the time I spent with Mr. Chase, memories that I have long since neglected and almost forgotten, flood my mind. Within each passing frame, I feel, see, hear the images fall bluntly.

It is a fall afternoon after school, and I'm lying stomach-down, legs dangling in the air and chin propped up by my hands, on the front entrance bench of Clarke Middle School. I am absorbed in my sixth-grade factoring homework while waiting for Mr. Chase to come. I have never met him, and truthfully, I'm a little dubious of this random man volunteering to teach me math on his own time. But when he comes in carrying his work briefcase and greets me with a serious, quiet expression, I feel a little more comfortable. We end up sitting in a small teacher's room talking about what I like and what he likes about math for the rest of the afternoon. Going home, I decide that maybe this won't be another restless math class filled with boring plug-and-chug problems. I like Mr. Chase, and I like talking about math with him.

Now Mr. Chase and I are in the same cramped teacher's room at the middle school on a dismal, rainy January afternoon. I'm at that little chalkboard (I wonder if it's still there?), scrawling numbers all over the place and he's sitting in a plastic chair too small for him. Only an eighth grader and just learning the complexities of math problem solving, I can't see the pattern in the numbers he's reading to me from a number theory book lying in his lap. He's smiling ever so slightly while watching me become frustrated. It takes us more than 30 minutes, but we reason the answer out together, slowly. By the time we finish, I'm excited, he's excited and we are pondering possible extensions of the pattern. I understand the whole proof!

I'm in high school now, freshman year. I've just blown into the room, a little late, and I plop into a seat front row center. Mr. Chase, at the whiteboard, is already explaining the math club's activity for the afternoon. Five minutes later, everyone else is busy puttering around with the materials, but Mr. Chase sits down with me and guides me through the exploration activity. I cut out the brightly colored tetrahedrons, octahedrons and dodecahedrons he has prepared ahead of time, and he directs me with questions about the number of edges, vertices and faces of each polyhedron. He leads me to conjecture a relationship between these three polyhedral characteristics, also known in texts as Euler's Theorem. When I look up momentarily, I see his smile—the special one I rarely glimpse—because he knows that I'm on the verge of making my conjecture.

A few months later, I'm at home, sitting on my bed, calling Mr. Chase. "Hello? Is Mr. Chase there?" A pause. "Hello?" His soft-spoken, scratchy, familiar voice comes on the line. I think I'm squealing by this point. "Guess what! I made the AIME!!" All our afternoons of hard work designing the best scoring strategies and exploring math problems has paid off, as I have qualified for the second level national math exam, the AIME. Chatting with him on the phone, I am excited to share the good news because we have reached our goal together.

A jolt. The moment has passed. Back in real time, I am stunned by the news of Mr. Chase's death. I am 17 years old, but this is the first time a person whom I knew well has passed away. Only thinking back now do I stop and fully appreciate the impact he made on my life. Only after he is gone do I realize that I, as well as so many other young mathematicians, have lost a great source of inspiration. I regret all those times in the past years that I thought of calling him to tell him about my latest mathematical endeavor but never quite got around to it. I wish I had called Mr. Chase to tell him about qualifying for the USAMO my junior year, the most pres-tigious national math exam, or making the elite 15-member state ARML team that took second place nationally. I want to thank him now for taking the time out of his busy work schedule to tutor me one-on-one in middle school and tell him that he was the person who first sparked my love for mathematics. In some way, though, I hope he knew how much he touched my life.

While I set the plastic polyhedra back into their dusty spot behind the dresser, I do not leave the memory of Mr. Chase hidden there with them as I once did a few years ago. Although I go on with my life, Mr. Chase is there. I reflect on Mr. Chase's generosity, gentleness, passion for math. I talk to my dad, math team coach and his other tutees about all the good conversations we had with him, joking around and thinking about math. I may have lost contact with Mr. Chase over the years, but playing with my old polyhedra set again freshly etched our relationship back into my mind, and his passing away has altered my formerly untouched perspective on life and death. As so aptly put to me by a friend during a recent conversation, "Welcome to life, Jackie."

Why This Essay Succeeded

This essay does several things right. First, Jackie introduces us to a person who was not only influential in her life but also the source of her greatest strength and academic passion. Second, while Jackie's subject is Mr. Chase, we actually learn more about her. It's her reactions to his lessons that are the heart of the essay and make it powerful. She even works in her own accomplishments in mathematics. Finally, Jackie shows us her ability to analyze her relationship with Mr. Chase throughout the years. She provides details when necessary but is also not afraid to time shift and take us from her past to the present in the span of a few sentences.

When writing an essay about an influential person—especially someone who is close to you—it is very easy to focus on the individual to extol all of his or her virtues. But you need to remember that the influential person is not applying to college—you are. This means the admission officers need to learn about you even if it is through your portrayal of another person.

Usbaldo Fraire, Jr.

San Antonio, Texas

Growing up in a single-parent family, Usbaldo describes his upbringing as one of poverty. But these challenges only motivated him to do more. While a student at Robert E. Lee High School, he mentored youth with similar backgrounds, encouraging them to resist joining gangs and to appreciate the value of education. He is the first in his family to attend college, and on top of that, he is helping to finance his own education as a national winner of the Hispanic Heritage Youth Award for Leadership.

Inspiration to Learn
University of Texas at Austin

In my family's past, no one has ever met the challenge of mathematics. In fact no one in my family has ever challenged anything because of their lack of education. My grandmother was illiterate when it came to complex math. Oppression limited her education to the third grade and simple addition and subtraction. My mother, aunts, uncles, along with my father never graduated or dared to attempt an algebra problem in school. The threat of x and y were too complex and overwhelming.

Over the years, I made up my mind to tackle mathematics. With some motivated teachers, I began to develop a keen interest in the subject. As a child I was always told that math was power, and power was what I wanted. So I took the challenge every year and thought of it as a game of "cracking the code," but I still had doubts about my abilities. I believed my understanding would end when I reached Algebra I, if I ever made it that far.

One day when I began to act up with other classmates, my social studies teacher Mr. Salinas pulled me out of class as he usually did and inevitably delivered a scolding. This time though I questioned his authority and asked why he never punished my friends, for they were guilty of the same nonsense. My train of thought completely changed when he said, "because I care about you." He began to explain that he had taught for 30 years at Gus Garcia Middle School and always looked for those students who had the potential to break our community's chain of failure. One day these students would come back to the barrio and prove that it was possible to become anything they wanted if they put the time and effort into their futures. He told me as though he strongly believed that I would be one of the students to accomplish this feat. He compared my math scores and overall grades to other students to show me that I was one of the top students of the school. Mr. Salinas made me believe until this day that I could break the chain of failure. His visions and expectations of me impacted the rest of my life; for the first time I had someone who believed in me passionately. He would bet his life on me, just as my mother would. His visions of me pointed my life in a positive direction.

Along with the support of my mother and grandmother, I was determined to make something of myself with mathematics. Mr. Salinas and my family made me set goals to challenge myself to the maximum and thus be able later to use my math skills for a successful job. During my senior year, I realized I wanted to expand my skills and learn more in order to study engineering. The rigorous courses of the University of Texas College of Engineering can help me accomplish my goals and in return I want to contribute to my society, building public schools, museums and libraries.

Why This Essay Succeeded

In this essay Usbaldo shares just one facet of a person who made an impact in his life. While he certainly had many interactions with his social studies teacher, the one that made a lasting impression was when Mr. Salinas explained why he singled out Usbaldo for discipline. The rest of the essay drives home the point that Usbaldo internalized from that single moment. Other students in this situation might have simply shrugged off their teacher's comment and continued with their behavior, but Usblado clearly made a transformation and the rest of his essay helps to substantiate this change.

Usbaldo's essay also does an excellent job of giving us an insight into his background. Showing us how little educational opportunities his family had and how troubled his community is helps us to put into context his achievements. This essay would be far less successful if Usbaldo came from a privileged family and attended an elite private school. Whatever your background—whether underprivileged or not—it's important to convey why your achievement is special. If you've overcome a challenge, say so.

Evelyn Thai
Van Nuys, California

Two things that are important to Evelyn are passion and honesty. As a student at Van Nuys High School, she participated in the things that satisfied those needs: political activism, community service and student government. As she was writing her admission essays, she adhered to her belief in the honest approach. She says, "I knew that as long as I was honest and was just being myself, I would get into the right school for me. And I was right. I love Princeton." She hopes to work in international relations or neurology.

A Fall from Grace
Princeton University

I pledge allegiance to the flag of the United States of America and to the Republic for which it stands, one nation under god, indivisible, with liberty and justice all.

Even though we don't even say it in school anymore, every morning I say this pledge to myself. Ever since I was little, I thought that the United States of America was the best place in the world—hey we had TWO Disneylands and don't forget that it was an American that had invented the Happy Meal. As I turned the path from scratch-kneed toddler into know-it-all seventh grader, being an American took on more meaning. My parents were refugees during the Vietnam War and it had been America that had saved them. For me, America stood for life, liberty, freedom, equality—all those characteristics Rousseau had once imagined possible in a country, all those characteristics America proudly touted in every children's history book. When the US went to war against Iraq, I didn't see it as an economically driven crusade, I thought that Saddam Hussein was really threatening my way of life and I hated him for being audacious enough to invade Kuwait. My perspective of the world fell roughly into two categories, good countries who agreed with the US and bad countries who didn't. The world worked like this and made sense because everything around me reinforced these ideas—from my elementary school teachers to our history books to everything on the nightly news.

Then I met Mister Pilloud. You have to spell it out, Mister Pilloud, because somehow Mister is more precise than Mr. If I close my eyes I can still remember every detail of Mister Pilloud's face. He had wrinkles at the corners of his eyes—little creases that angled upward, not from old age but smiles. What I remember most distinctly about the man is that he always smelled like day-old coffee. He had coffee every day—two, three, ten cups were never too many. This coffee addict wasn't even really my teacher. A student teacher would teach us while he supervised.

Yet the best times were when the student teacher was absent. Mister Pilloud would begin by recounting to us what he called a horrible story. The horrible story would then turn out to be something in the news that was going on while we spoke. The classroom was never more alive, my peers never as thoughtful and as enraptured as in those 52 minutes when Mister Pilloud spoke. At first, when he told me that our government was dumping millions of gallons of milk away so that the milk industry wouldn't suffer losses, I didn't believe him. I refused to believe that my country, such a great and caring country, could be so wasteful while there were all these people starving in countries around the world. So I looked it up and saw that he was not lying.

Thus it went for over a year, and when he was no longer my teacher, I would go talk to him at lunch. Hussein didn't turn into an angel, but the United States of America began to fall from grace. My whole ideal system began to crumble and I learned that the world is not black and white. Mister Pilloud taught me that you can't always believe what you read and that the truth is out there for me to discover. He made me realize that it was not our country that I love. I love everything that our country is supposed to stand for.

Why This Essay Succeeded

Evelyn's essay illustrates her perceptiveness and thoughtfulness. Instead of simply describing Mister Pilloud, she shows us how she has changed from this experience. We learn how naive she was—which in itself is a very mature observation. Then we meet Mister Pilloud and we can actually see what he looks (and smells) like. All of this helps us to develop a mental image of this person.

While describing Mister Pilloud's lessons of questioning the conventional wisdom, what really makes an impact is the end of the essay when we get to see an "after" view of Evelyn. No longer naive and unquestioning, she is now a sophisticated and critical thinker. By the end of the essay we have a much better idea of one aspect of Evelyn's personality and we can see how she has become the person she is.

Memorable Essay: Cracking Your Brain Open

Director of admission, Harvey Mudd College and former associate dean of admission, Pomona College

You don't need to find an event that could only happen to you to have an original essay. In fact, everyday incidents make great subjects. What will make your essay unique and original is how you approach the subject and the quality of your analysis.

Peter Osgood, director of admission at Harvey Mudd College and former associate dean of admission at Pomona College, remembers one essay that "blew everyone away" at Pomona. What was so impressive was not the subject of the essay but how the student analyzed it.

Osgood recalls that the student wrote an essay on a very everyday topic. She was with some friends and some things were said that shouldn't have been said. He says, "Feelings were hurt. We've all been in these situations before. But what this student did was very astutely analyze the situation. She cracked open her brain like a coconut. It was a powerful and thought-provoking essay."

Don't give yourself a permanent migraine trying to come up with the one-and-only-original-topic when you can usually take something mundane and through your analysis and presentation make it into a powerful essay.

Cecilia A. Oleck

Grand Rapids, Michigan

If there is one lesson that Cecilia has learned, it's the importance of listening. Her teacher? A doll named Christopher, which she describes as the one item she planned to take to college. Cecilia understands the importance of listening, not only in her personal life but in her professional future as well. She plans to become a journalist. At West Catholic High School, she wrote for the newspaper, tackling topics such as the double standards for athletes and gender stereotypes. She is now a student at Saint Mary's College in South Bend, Indiana.

Christopher
Northwestern University

When I leave for college, among my belongings will be an item not so unusual as it is beloved. Along with the normal objects for daily life will be my most precious possession, my Cabbage Patch doll Christopher. Christopher and I have been virtually inseparable since my first year of life, nearly 18 years ago.

I think he is adorable. He has coarse, brown hair made of yarn, a smooth plastic face and warm brown eyes. He wears a never-fading smile and has a soft body. Christopher is dressed in blue jeans and a blue and white striped shirt.

This doll has been a great comfort to me throughout the trials of my life. I remember when I was younger and got upset about something, I would always get Christopher and trace his face with my fingers. His face is cool and smooth and I was always relaxed by the simple motion. I find myself using this calming technique to this day.

Christopher has also seen his share of hardships. In two unrelated yet unfortunate accidents, he lost a leg and then an arm, both of which my mom lovingly sewed back on. He has also suffered from a head wound, a crack in the skull, from a careless cousin slamming him against a headboard. My dad acted as a surgeon for this emergency and soon Christopher was back on his feet. The scar from that operation is still visible in the form of glue. While some might think that this detracts from Christopher's physical beauty, I feel it adds to his character.

Christopher has been present for all the major milestones in my life, as well as for the monotony of daily life. We have traveled to many different places together. We have visited family in New Jersey, New York and Tennessee, vacationed in Florida, Texas, Mexico and Mackinaw Island. We've been to summer camps together and we also were able to explore the western part of the United States with 30 of my classmates. I did have to leave Christopher at home when I went on a mission trip to Costa Rica this past summer. I was worried that he might not survive the trip and I was not willing to risk losing him.

Sometimes I find myself wondering why I would form such a strong attachment for an inanimate object, as I am not a very materialistic person. I honestly cannot answer that question. As I reflect on all that has happened to me in my young life, I realize that this simple doll has helped me to learn some valuable lessons. It is always nice to know that I have someone who will be there no matter what I do. I remember when I was younger. I would talk to Christopher and tell him everything. He would do nothing more than sit there smiling at me. He is not human, so he was never shocked at my revelations and he never scolded me or offered me advice. He just listened.

It has taken me 18 years to begin to understand the concept of just listening. It was one of the healthiest things for me to be able to vent my frustrations or share my excitements without being interrupted. I see now how the people that I am involved with need that as well. I have discovered that I do not need to always talk to make an impact but by listening to a person I may help someone the most.

Christopher's unusualness comes from everything he has been through. I think the most important thing that I have realized from having Christopher is to keep and cherish the reminders of my childhood with me for the rest of my life. There is an innocence and beauty to children that many people seem to lose as they become adults. I am ready to take on more responsibilities in my life and I do not shrink from my independence and from growing up, but I still want to keep some of those childlike qualities alive inside of me. Every time I look at Christopher I am reminded of that.

Why This Essay Succeeded

Who says an influential person has to be human? Cecilia redefines the question so that it fits her own experience. This is a very creative approach and works not because we are surprised to learn that Christopher is a doll but because Cecilia is able to convince us why this doll has been so significant.

Through her essay, Cecilia explains how Christopher has been the one constant in her life and has served as a source of strength and comfort. The ability to recognize and convey this idea in her essay shows her ability to think and examine. A good essay is a synthesis of both writing and analytical abilities.

Things That Represent Me

Linda Lau
Flushing, New York

Linda says that a creative essay question makes her think philosophically. So when Cornell asked her to describe three important objects, she reflected on three Looney Tunes characters. These three animals taught her the value of working hard, how to express herself through music and art and the meaning of dreams. She developed these values while a student at Stuyvesant High School, where she was involved in yearbook and orchestra. Linda also participated in the Hong Kong Dragon Boat Festival.

A Dog, a Cat and a Bird
Cornell University

I remember years ago, I loved watching the Looney Tunes with Tweetie bird, Sylvester the cat and the bulldog. The plot seemed always the same. Sylvester would try to eat the bird, which would then either outsmart him, hide or seek protection from the dog. That was hardly my favorite show but the three animals involved quite impressively influenced my philosophy of life. I believe that as one grows and develops, it is possible for a human to have seemingly contradictory potentials, values and attributes. As a result of these different layers of personality, we can develop into certain "perfect" characters. I find in these three animals some distinct characteristics that I have and wish to possess.

In Chinese culture there is a belief that a person is born into a state of being determined by the exact geo-temporal dimension of birth. Not intending to restrict a person's abilities, this determination supposedly foretells the characteristics and potentials contained within the person. In my case, by the lunar calendar, I was born in the year of the dog, signifying that I would be a diligent, devoted, straightforward and friendly person. Whether or not I am who I am because of the year I was born into, or rather the self-fulfilled prophesy created through my own belief that is what I should be, I have indeed turned out to be a devoted hard worker. I may at times be considered stubborn as well. Thinking back, I have indeed spent my first few years in love with dogs. It is one of my favorite animals though I still do not own one, if the one within me is not counted.

I believe I started to like cats a few years after my family picked up a black and white stray cat. The reason for the long lead time was not because of my previous affection for dogs but mainly because of the fear I had of cats. Extremely clever and in control, the dignified animal does at times seem to be very independent and unperturbed by its surroundings. However, cats will cling on to people they trust. And once a bond is established, it hardly ever breaks unless of course, there is total betrayal. There is perhaps a streak of wildness trapped within cats; that they cannot be entirely tamed sometimes makes them pretty dangerous. However, their frankness and show-all emotion is the reason for my liking them. To watch the actions and manners of my cat, whether sleeping cozily on my bed or speeding crazily through the halls, refreshes me like cool breezes in the heat of a summer's day. In my opinion, a cat's body language speaks volumes in comparison to human words. Perhaps this is why I would rather express myself through music and art than words, because as descriptive or symbolic as words can be, they may not convey true feelings or meanings that are intended.

One day, my cat came back after a walk and presented to my family a dead bird. At that time, my entire family felt shocked and puzzled, but I now know that for the cat the lifeless gift signified his disposition and trust towards us. Coming from an innate instinct, birds were his prey. Catching a bird is his dream come true, a rite-de-passage for his cathood. As fast as birds can glide and as high as they can soar, when the time comes, they are still not quick enough. For me, birds remind me of the goal in front of me that is forever flickering but elusive. I don't have intrinsic powers to catch "birds." However, like dreams, they are things so fast and beautiful that I hesitate to catch them even if I can for fear that if I do and successfully cage one, it will no longer be the bird I cherished.

In the cartoon, the dog, the cat and the bird coexisted together because they shared the same space and were forced to live together. They are able to grow to adore and aid one other despite their varying personalities. Correspondingly, I believe that when a person is given the chance to intermingle with others, however idiosyncratic, it may turn out that new and loyal bonds would be established. Life may not always be mischievous chasing, bullying or outsmarting each other after all.

Why This Essay Succeeded

Linda takes a risk by attempting to connect a Looney Tunes cartoon with ancient Chinese philosophy. At first this seems odd but Linda is successful because she ties the characters to her own philosophy and experiences. Her analysis is multifaceted. For example, she addresses both the literal connections between the cartoon cat and her own cat as well as the less overt shared personality traits between her cat and herself.

Using the cartoon as a metaphor for her personality—she is loyal and hard working like a dog, expressive through the arts like a cat and reaching for goals like a cat does for birds—Linda gives a great deal of insight into what kind of person she is. This, after all, is the point of all college admission essays. You need to reveal something about yourself. That Linda is able to do this through weaving her own traits with that of the animals—both real and animate—is only more impressive.

Gabriel D. Carroll

For this essay, Stanford asked applicants to include a photo of something important to them and write about it. Gabriel's photo was of paper.

Paperboy
Stanford University

At an age when my friends' floors were strewn with toys, dirty clothes or video-game cartridges, mine was smothered in paper of all sorts—books, magazines, reams of white and college-ruled, paper bags, paper airplanes. This pattern has survived, and it is representative of the way I live. The house of my life is built on a foundation of paper.

Certainly this element is crucial in all our lives. From money to facial tissues to news to playing cards, paper is a vital organ of the body politic. And I, as a student, laden with schoolwork (and college application forms), should naturally expect to be particularly prone. But, for me, paper goes even beyond this role. Virtually all of my favorite activities are paper-based. I compose music, poetry and prose. I do mathematics, with massive scratchwork as a by-product. I solve cryptic crosswords. Last year, I was involved in CX debate, which may be cynically but not inaccurately said to consist essentially of reading prepared pieces of paper in a strategically determined order. To me, paper is the natural medium for connecting the mind—whether in its imaginative, mechanical, or emotive capacity—with the physical world. Small wonder, then, that I find I express myself more effectively in writing than in speech, or that, on my habitual multiple-hour walks, I often carry blank paper and pens to jot down any arbitrary thoughts that might seem worthy of retention.

Even beyond this, my intimate relationship with paper extends to some unorthodox functions. I have developed a rudimentary silent communication system with friends, involving holding up sheets of various colors. When it comes to cleaning up spills, I far prefer the use of paper towels over sponges. At the age of 13, I caused myself some jaw trouble through excessive use of paper as a substitute for chewing gum, though I have largely overcome that habit. In prescribing the role of paper, I can be picky—college-ruled, never wide-ruled, because more words fit on the former—but I can also be flexible—using napkins to scribble visual aids during mealtime conversation.

But as significant as what I chose for this photograph is what I did not choose. Fancier objects would have been inappropriate, because ostentatious materialism is meaningless to me. Sure, a few of the habits I have acquired require more expensive materials—programming is difficult to do and impossible to do usefully in the absence of a computer; likewise for chess without a board or pieces—but, for the most part, my interests require little more than scribbling equipment. I am a believer in resourcefulness. Do as much as you can with the facilities at your disposal, I say. Hence, armed with paper and pens, I can (in theory) keep myself entertained all day. In the mathematical world, greater value is attached to a proof of a difficult theorem if it uses only the most elementary techniques; perhaps my inheritance of this esthetic is reflected in my preference for building a life from the simple tools of paper and pens. I spurn more elaborate equipment. Why use a calculator when you can do computations in your head? Reading information from computer screens bothers me; I prefer to print things out, or simply to use books. I would rather simply proofread my own writing than rely on automated spell-checkers. And my dependence on paper embodies not only resourcefulness but thrift. I rarely buy new clothes. I use public transit (or walk), which appears especially frugal in light of today's gasoline prices. Paper, being plentiful and inexpensive, fits into this scheme. Recently, I took this trait to a new height: whereas I previously sent paper to the recycle bin after depleting one side, I now make a conscious effort to use both sides of every sheet, thus saving on future purchases.

Paper is the staple of my existence (no pun intended). From when I was 6 and spent my days filling pads with fantastical designs for houses, zoos and factories, to the present, when I surround myself with sheets bearing drafts of essays on one side and systems of equations on the other, my life has been ruled by this ruled substance—simple, utile and ubiquitous.

Why This Essay Succeeded

Part of the magic of Gabriel's essay is his ability to find the one common thread that binds his world. Recognizing the importance of paper probably took Gabriel longer than it took to write the actual essay. But paper is the perfect metaphor for who he is.

Gabriel adeptly conveys why paper is so important. He works in his interests from composing music to debating to communicating with friends. He is also able to describe his values of resourcefulness and thrift. His essay is not just about the things he does but also what he believes. By the end of his essay we have a clear mental image of the kind of person Gabriel is and we fully believe that given a pad of paper and pens he could keep himself occupied all day.

Marie A. McKiernan

Warwick, New York

A dancer and pianist since elementary school, Marie has won four Professional Dance Teacher's Association and Hoctor Dance bronze medals and taught children how to dance. She shares her interests, which include dancing and her love of potatoes, in her essay about three objects. At John S. Burke Catholic High School, she volunteered with the National Honor Society and worked in a dental office to explore a possible future in that field.

A Potato, a Seashell, a Pair of Eyeglasses
Cornell University

A potato, a seashell, a pair of eyeglasses; all three of these small objects offer a window into my personality. I can assure you that I do not picture myself as a round, dirty carbohydrate, a leftover from an oyster dinner or the spectacles from the dollar store my mother seems to constantly misplace; rather, these three objects reveal my versatility, my inner character and my ability to discern different perspectives.

Oddly enough, a potato reveals much about me. I love potatoes. Mashed, baked, broiled, fried or roasted, potatoes are delicious. The versatility seen in the preparation of this vegetable parallels my own versatile interests. On any given day I may find myself choreographing a dance to a new Latin rhythm, discussing calculus with a peer, playing classical music with my father or making greeting cards with a new stamp I purchased. There is no limit to the possibilities. I believe this versatility allows me to be open to new experiences and enables me to adapt to these fresh situations. In addition, like the roots of the potato that grow deep into the ground, the foundation of my character, such as honesty, integrity, compassion and my Catholic faith, are deeply rooted in who I am.

The potato alone only reveals a part of me, so I add the seashell as a representative of another aspect of myself. The seashell's true beauty and potential lie deep within its channels. One must hold the shell to his or her ear and listen carefully to understand the seashell's immensity. Similarly, my true potential and inner character lie within me. Therefore, I must listen carefully to my conscience and soul to achieve all I am capable of accomplishing. If I stay true to my values such as truthfulness, humility and kindness, I can reach my greatest ability and personal success. This may include believing in myself when struggling with a new tap step or following my heart and dream of one day becoming a dentist. The seashell reminds me to listen and believe in who I am.

Although the potato and the seashell reveal a majority of who I am, I would be remiss in not mentioning the value of spectacles. I have been cursed with poor eyesight for the majority of my academic career. However, this malady has proved to be a blessing in disguise. My ailing vision introduced me to eyeglasses. Eyeglasses come in a myriad of sizes, shapes, shades and prescriptions; however, they do not singly represent one's visual handicap or personal style. These possibilities reflect differing perspectives of sight and life. When I equip myself with spectacles, a window of perspective opens to me. My vague, fuzzy world transforms allowing me to see another perspective. Although my physical vision is limited, I do not allow my vision of the world to be distorted. When I do feel that I am constricting my view, I revert to my eyeglasses, my window of perspective and all which I have yet to brave.

A potato, a seashell, a pair of eyeglasses; each of these objects reveals a truth about me. I am a person who desires to indulge in varied experiences, a person who continually tries to be true to herself and a person who quests to see the world in all its colors. These objects bring me back to my reality and fuel my determination for my future.

Why This Essay Succeeded

The introduction to an essay is very important because it entices the admission officers, drawing them into the story and making them want to read to the end. Don't you want to know how these three seemingly disparate objects—a potato, seashell and eyeglasses—are reflective of Marie?

Notice how Marie defines each object in a way that helps her illustrate her personality. The potato is "versatile" while the seashell displays "inner character" and the spectacles not only represent her poor eyesight but her ability to see different "perspectives." Whatever you write about, you don't have to use the literal or conventional definition. Feel free to be creative and interpret things the way you want to. Remember, it's your essay and you are in control. The reader is just along for the ride.

Adam Bayne Hopkins

Dallas, Texas

"I'd like to be the absolute best in one range of study," says Adam. And he identifies that area as physics. At Greenhill School, he was awarded the Bausch and Lomb Fellowship for being the best science student in his school and the Physics/Pre-Calculus Student Award. Adam was also captain of the varsity soccer team and participated in weights, boxing and lacrosse. In this essay, he answers Princeton's Hodge-Podge question, providing brief but insightful answers about what he likes outside of physics as well.

Hodge-Podge
Princeton University

Favorite book: King Rat (James Clavell)

Favorite recording: Sunburn (Fuel)

Favorite movie: Cruel Intentions

Favorite TV program: Star Trek, The Next Generation

Favorite source of news: New York Times, Dallas Morning News

Favorite way to relax: Play soccer/juggle soccer ball, play the piano

Favorite time of the year: Winter

Favorite food: Cheese fries

Favorite place to get away from it all: My car

Two adjectives your friends would use to describe you: Intense, devoted

A pet peeve of yours: Sometimes people just don't stop talking

The best advice you've ever received: "Always do your best and work your hardest." (My dad)

Why This Essay Succeeded

As you can tell, this was a short answer question, which allowed Adam to be creative by using a list instead of an essay. (Adam did write a more traditional essay for the longer questions that Princeton asked.) This is an excellent example of how the quality of thinking, rather than the writing, is what makes an essay successful. Each of Adam's answers appears both genuine and descriptive of who he is. For example, Adam's responses suggest that he is a science fiction fan who is intense but has room for creative outlets. He has selected favorite things that really show different sides of his personality, making him an interesting person to the admission officers. Like many of the essays in this book, it took Adam a lot longer to conceive this essay than to actually write it.

Memorable Essay: Spaghetti Sauce
Dean of Undergraduate Admission, Case Western Reserve University

"I remember reading a great essay and then running from door to door telling everyone they had to read it," says William T. Conley, dean of undergraduate admission at Case Western Reserve University, recalling an outstanding essay he read recently.

What made the essay memorable was the way the writer compared his life to an everyday food: spaghetti sauce. The student wrote about how he had once seen an old commercial for Ragu spaghetti sauce in which a chef talks about all of the fresh vegetables and spices that went into the sauce. Conley says, "The writer wrote about himself by cleverly drawing parallels between the spaghetti sauce and the ingredients that make up his personality. He handled the analogy extremely well. It was very impressive."

Writing a creative essay like this is not easy. It takes a lot of thinking to be able to compare yourself to something in an intelligent and meaningful way. You can't just draw parallels to surface similarities. (Spaghetti sauce looks good in red and so do I.) You need to go deeper. Doing so successfully can yield a powerful essay. Who knows, maybe your essay will be the one that Conley holds in his hand the next time he runs through his office.

Emily Heikamp

"Why"
University of Virginia

My favorite word annoyed my parents when I was small, and continues to puzzle my teachers today. In fact, it has baffled the greatest minds of all time. This word is responsible for the birth of every religion, and the entire discipline of science is based on this single syllable. Authors, artists and scholars have attempted to explain this word, but each has given a different interpretation. Although it is quite a basic word, complexity lies in its simplicity. When used alone, it may pose a question that many find difficult to answer. This word is also unique, as it is one of the few grammatonyms of the English language (a word that sounds like a letter of the alphabet). It is also a popular word and has even appeared on this very application.

My favorite word is "why." Throughout my life, I have always asked why things happen or even why I must clean my room. "Why" represents a thirst for knowledge and has been an essential part of my education and my life. Asking "why" has produced new ideas and explanations, whereas those who do not inquire "why" must be satisfied with superficial facts. "Why" has given me reasons for working hard, for believing in myself, for applying to U.V.A. and even for my very existence. I shall never stop asking my favorite word, "why."

Why This Essay Succeeded

In a very brief space, Emily successfully shares an important side of her personality. Clearly this is only one aspect but from the college's perspective it is probably one of the most significant. Colleges like to see that students are interested in learning and gaining knowledge not because they have to but because they want to. Emily's essay leaves no doubt that she is passionate about learning more about the world around her.

In at least one of your essays, try to address your academic or intellectual curiosity. What have you enjoyed studying most in high school? What would you like to study in college? What intellectual questions keep you up at night? By sharing this kind of information, you will reinforce to the college that you are ready for the academic rigors.

Essays About Writing Essays

Misty M. Haberer
Temple, Texas
At first Misty was stumped on what to write about for her essay. After quizzing her friends about their essay topics, she realized that inspiration needed to come from herself. "I wasn't them and I was only myself," she says. A graduate of Temple High School, Misty was a National Merit Finalist, captain of the school's dance/drill team and violinist in the orchestra. Fluent in French, she hopes to teach foreign language. Misty wrote this essay to first gain admission to Southern Methodist University as a freshman and then to transfer to Southwestern University.

The Great Search
Southwestern University

It seems that there should be a better inspiration for attempting a well-written, succinct college application essay than bathroom towels. Life is full of surprises! I puzzled for several weeks over how to objectively and un-obtrusively make myself look like Superwoman in 500 words or less to the people who have control over my course of action for the next four years. Hoping to smash the writer's block, I turned to my friends.

One had written a pity-inducing narrative of her 2,000-mile trek to a new state and the resulting rise in confidence and self-esteem at a new high school. Having lived in the same house for the better part of my life, this would not work for me. There was the girl who, sitting in detention for breaking the dress code, wrote a scathing criticism of the bureaucracy of the American school system. This wouldn't do either, since I have a rather consistent habit (good or bad, depending on how you look at it) of respecting even the most arbitrary of rules. Next in The Great Search came my feminist friend who wrote a victorious expository on becoming the first female member of Temple High School's Key Club. Despite being a pro-gender-equality, quasi-feminist, I quite honestly didn't care whether Shannon Faulkner was accepted into the Citadel, so I couldn't use that topic either.

Finally, in my effort to produce what admission teams deem an acceptable essay, I uncovered the great inspiration of the bathroom towels. An Ivy League-worthy friend, after noticing the basket of flowers design on her bathroom towels, wrote a brilliant essay comparing the intricacies of her personality to an intricate yet unfinished woven basket. Pensively, I analyzed this concept. I was convinced the secret to an incredible essay was dangling from the wall in my bathroom. Rather pathetically, I actually went home and stared at them. Unfortunately, my writing skills were not stimulated by the solid burgundy towels hanging innocently from their hooks.

Panicking by this point because the essay was due in, yes, three days, I recounted my Great Search to yet another friend. She laughed and said, "Misty, instead of worrying over what to write, why don't you write about worrying over what to write?" The Great Search was over; the answer had been found. I felt rather stupid that the answer had been so obvious. I suppose, however, that is the "Essence of Misty." I start out confused. Then I worry. Panic sets in. Just in time, I discover the solution and I always get it done. I am the driver who hates to be told where to go. I know where I'm going, or at least claim to know, and although I have individualistic ways of getting there it makes life more interesting. And, I am an individual. As I have observed my peers over the last few years, I've noticed that daily life has become a game of mirrors. Everyone is a reflection of someone else. Soon the reflections become more important than the people themselves. I refuse to mirror others, and my many idiosyncrasies prove it.

Paradoxically, I have managed to describe myself in an essay primarily concerned with complaining about having to describe myself. From the pity-inducing narrative, to the scathing criticism, to the victorious expository, to the inspiration of the bathroom towels, that is how I objectively and unobtrusively present myself to you.

Why This Essay Succeeded

Believe it or not, writing about the process of writing your college admission essay is a popular topic. It may seem original to you, but trust us: Thousands of other applicants are thinking the same. Fortunately, Misty avoids the common pitfalls of this topic by revealing a lot about herself in the essay. And she proves that any topic—no matter how common—can be made original with the right approach.

If you insist on writing about the essay or any other part of the admission process, follow Misty's example. No, you don't have to sit and stare at your bathroom towels. Just be original and be yourself. That's what the exercise is all about.

Extracurricular Activities and Athletics

Samantha J. Cooper
New York, New York
A heartbreaking injury forced Samantha to reevaluate her future as a dancer. In her essay, she describes how she dealt with the decision that she says "changed the course of (her) life." At Horace Mann High School, Samantha was editor of the school's weekly newspaper, president of the Shakespeare Club and governor of the Northeastern State in the Junior State of America, the highest elected student position. She plans to work in journalism or law.

How Podiatry Begat Oratory
Princeton University

The os trigonum is largely unknown outside dance circles. As its Latin name suggests, it is a bone of triangular shape, typically equilateral. It is found at the base of the ankle and is no greater than two centimeters in size. Like its better-known anatomical counterparts, the tonsils and appendix, this vestigial bone is an evolutionary dead end. My very personal discovery of it forced me to reevaluate my dance career and to seek application of its lessons elsewhere.

My summers were spent dancing at the Saratoga Performing Arts Center since Madam's stick came to rest at my side. Madam was one of several French-speaking pre-Soviet Russian ballet mistresses. Each mistress had a prized talent, the ability to select from many the few to whom they would impart the collective wisdom of Petipa, Balanchine and Robbins. I met Madam and first spied her stick at an annual carnival of tears, the auditions for the School of American Ballet, teaching affiliate of the New York City Ballet. Places in the school's pre-professional program were so coveted that any applicant's chance of admission is less than slight. I was 8 and I thought Madam's stick prevented her from toppling, but now I understand that her stick was a divining rod. It navigated a sea of pink satin and then came to rest near a few modestly nourished hopefuls.

The stick found me, and joy reigned in our previously danceless household. Family and school schedules would now accommodate my group classes, private classes, auditions and performances. Three hundred "Nutcracker" performances at a nonunion $9 each and an assortment of "Sleeping Beauties" and "Midsummer Night's Dreams," followed with increasingly demanding roles and stage time. I joined the company's trips to the capital district in summer and returned to Lincoln Center for fall season. On stage or off, I was defined by teachers, friends and relatives in terms of art. I was a dancer-student, dancer-daughter and dancer-sister. I saw myself the same way, and I thought this identity would endure. All changed that summer when local specialists, Advil and cortisone failed to quiet the superfluous bone. A surgeon helped the fractured "os," and life as a ballerina in training had ended. Nature had betrayed me. While recovering, I replayed Madam's classes and searched for lessons that could be salvaged and applied to other aspects of my life. I was too young to be known for what I used to do.

The bone departed, but the relevance of the lessons remained. From a young age dance instilled discipline, focus and determination, skills no less valuable today. In learning choreography, I became analytical, searching for meaning in movement just as words convey feelings in poetry. I could communicate with the last row of any arena through pacing, cadence and rhythm. Ballet was my unconventional prerequisite for political debate, journalism and Shakespeare. When I joined Junior State of America (JSA) the gavel on the podium became my siren as Madam's stick upon the hardwood. In JSA the theatre is a convention center and the audience is filled with constituents. My instrument is now my voice and the message my improvisation. In dance, I learned to move in unison with partners, excellent preparation for diplomacy. I play to the back rows to use the skills Madam taught to inspire others to collaborate as a unified corps.

While I have succumbed to the lures of the newspaper, JSA and Shakespeare with satisfaction and fulfillment, I still think of Madam's stick and her lessons that have served me well in all my pursuits. As I stride confidently to the front of the ballroom to open debate conventions, whether in Boston, Stamford or Washington, D.C., I can still hear Madam reminding me, "Shoulders down. Chin up. Project!"

Why This Essay Succeeded

One of the strengths of Samantha's essay is the story. She shares the tale of her celebrated selection to the School of American Ballet, her rise as a dancer and her horrific fall. And after all of this, she explains what she has learned from the experience. Who wouldn't be moved by her experience? But even if you haven't had such a traumatic occasion, you can see how it helps to be self-analytical and convey what you have gained from participation in an activity.

The other strength of this essay, and we can't say this enough for all of you, is the quality of her writing. Samantha creates a vivid illustration of Madam, the celebration after being selected and her resulting experience in JSA. She picks and chooses just the right details to share without overloading the essay with unnecessary descriptions. A good writer is economical with words—using only those that are absolutely essential to the story. This is especially true with the limited space of a college admission essay.

Donald H. Matsuda, Jr.

Sacramento, California

Even though he knew that his work inside of the classroom was important, Donald placed a high priority on his contributions outside the classroom as well. At Jesuit High School, Donald was editor of the newspaper and yearbook, director of counselors at Camp ReCreation, a summer camp for mentally and physically disabled children, and president of his church's youth group. He says, "It's satisfying to see I can make a difference." Donald plans to obtain M.D. and M.P.H. degrees.

California Boys' State
Stanford University

My tired eyes managed to slowly glide across the bright paper, struggling to distinguish the fading black type: "You have been distinguished as the top in the junior class...in terms of leadership, character and scholastic ability." I certainly felt honored to be recognized for my diligence throughout my high school career, although I was uncertain as to what this nomination was for. I continued, my ambivalence apparent by the expression on my face, until I discovered the two words which explained it all: Boys' State.

I was informed that I would have to be interviewed, the opportunity for me to present the genuine "who I am" as opposed to "what I have done." Numerous past achievements are undoubtedly essential in the evaluation of an individual, but as philosopher Ralph Waldo Emerson once sagely observed, "What lies behind us and what lies before us are small matters compared to what lies within us."

Once the interviews were completed and our records were reviewed (there were three other candidates who were nominated), the only thing left to do was wait. (This is, other than attending to the rigors of our engaged high school lives.) I was soon informed that I would represent Jesuit High School at California Boys' State. I was ecstatic! I have always been eager to pursue and gain experience in any field of knowledge. Thus this opportunity was very intellectually promising. Nonetheless, my stay at Boys' State was not at all as I had anticipated it to be.

The week commenced rather quickly as all of the delegates nervously arrived from various areas of California, most having adjusted to dormitory-style living within a matter of hours. All of the boys, divided into more productive groups termed "cities," gradually united to build their own municipal governments. I spent the first few hours frantically studying for the afternoon bar examination, which ultimately deemed me proficient to practice law. Once the tension from the examination slowly dissipated, I was able to spend a considerable amount of time acquainting myself with some of the most outstanding fellow leaders in the state. This, undoubtedly, was one of the most remarkable aspects of Boys' State. I was given the opportunity to meet these talented scholars and to learn about their academic and personal lives. I imagined it to be somewhat similar to orientation week at a very prestigious university (such as Stanford), for the most brilliant minds and talents convened on one campus. Each individual strove for the best but was always primed to work with others for the betterment of our city. This was unlike anything I had ever experienced at the high school level, and I must admit, it was wonderfully refreshing. Nevertheless, socializing with others was only a minor aspect of the complete experience. We were faced with numerous challenges of establishing efficient city and county governments, building successful political campaigns and presenting speeches.

Eight days passed more rapidly than the fleeting days of summer. Nevertheless, I felt that we, as a city, worked hard to accomplish all that we possibly could in one week. The opportunities that I was afforded (my election to the treasurer position, actively participating in running our city government and receiving the Most Outstanding Model City Award) were accomplishments that were achieved through the efforts of everyone in our city. The teamwork was absolutely remarkable. I will treasure the moments which were spent sharing knowledge, ideas and experiences with my roommates. It was incredible that, within a short period of time, our city of 40 strangers had bonded so beautifully and developed friendships for life.

Although Boys' State was an intensive week of practical political science, it offered so much more than just training for a life of playing "the power game," as author Hedrick Smith termed it. I gained a wealth of new knowledge about government and efficiency, countless friendships and, most importantly, a newfound outlook on life. While it seems incomprehensible that eight days could make such a profound difference in one's life, I now believe it can. I did not just come away from my stay as a well-informed United States citizen. I feel that I emerged a leader, ready and willing to take the invaluable experiences of Boys' State and make a contribution to my high school, my community and my prospective college. I am now able to appreciate the importance of the qualities which constitute a true leader—responsibility, charisma, efficiency and, most importantly, honesty. My one week was well spent in that I also experienced a taste of what college is about: learning from textbooks, professors, friends, roommates and experience.

It would be an understatement to reflect upon this week as an "experience of a lifetime" because it was so significant to me. It was an experience that was beyond my expectations and one which I will certainly continue to build upon.

Why This Essay Succeeded

When writing about an experience, it's important to not only tell what happened but to explain its effect on you. Donald conveys a clear picture of the hectic week that he spent at Boys' State, but he also interprets the lessons he learned about leadership and political science during the time. More important than what he did is what he gained from the experience.

For this type of essay, it's important to remember to explain what you have discovered. The lesson doesn't have to reveal the "secret of life." It can be something small that you had not realized before. Using specific incidents is also helpful. You don't have to be able to write complex prose to create a good essay. Simply having an eye for detail and presenting your thesis in a clear, uncluttered style can yield a successful essay.

Kathleen C. Degen

Narberth, Pennsylvania

When she was writing her application essays, Kathleen knew that her strong academic record could speak for itself. She wanted to show the colleges another side of her. "I tried to write about things that were truly important to me in hopes of giving the admission officers a feel for what I was like outside of my grades and test scores," she says. Kathleen was the captain of the varsity squash and crew teams and participated in theatre and the literary magazine at the Episcopal Academy.

On the Water
Princeton University

In the words of a former teammate, "Crew teaches you to find your limits and then surpass them." There is no better feeling than finishing a 60-minute piece weary, exhausted and totally drained of energy knowing that you and your teammates have put your absolute all and more into it. The sport often entails early practices, late practices, long practices, hot weather, cold weather, blistered hands and general discomfort. Nevertheless, when you feel like you could not possibly force your legs up the slide one more time, the eventual goal of making that next piece or next race that much better pushes you to keep going and take another stroke.

Crew has also been one of the most humbling and rewarding experiences for me. I began the sport knowing virtually nothing about it. I now have a profound sense of what it is like to work towards a common goal with a group of people and, in the process, develop meaningful friendships. I have learned that it is impossible to succeed if all eight rowers do not work together. There are no stars. Unless the rowers think of themselves as one boat as opposed to eight individuals, it is simply not possible to win. It has taught me a life lesson that there is no way one can make it solely on her own and that sometimes it is necessary to seek help and support even when independence is what she may desire.

Why This Essay Succeeded

You often have a very limited space in which to write about an activity. Yet, Kathleen effectively describes why she has a passion for crew and what she has gained from the experience. She allows the admission officers to get inside her head to understand her motivations. When writing a short essay about an activity, it's critical to select a specific aspect. Don't try to cover all 12 reasons why you enjoy crew. Instead, zero in on one or two that are the most important. This will allow you, as Kathleen has done, to write a meaningful essay using only a couple of paragraphs.

Michelle Lloyd
Dallas, Texas

There are a few things about Michelle that might surprise you. You probably wouldn't expect someone who is passionate about electrical engineering to also be enthused by piano, dance and poetry. But Michelle has talents in these disparate areas. A graduate of The Hockaday School, she was a National Merit Scholar and perhaps even more significantly actually enjoyed writing her essay. She says, "I think it is a valuable exercise to sift back through your own personal experiences and see how they have affected who you are and what you want to become." She may work in engineering, linguistics or academia.

Gordito
Rice University

"¡Gordito! ¡Gordito!" they teased as he jumped rope, but Ivan did not seem to mind being called chubby because he continued to enjoy himself and the company of the other children in the parking lot. His not-so-white shirt has a little tear and some dirt smudged on it, but he blended in with the other children playing at our Backyard Bible Club. Some, like Ivan, had worn the same outfit each day that our choir had come to the apartment complexes with our games, crafts, songs and stories. As part of our mission trip to Mexico City, we wanted to reach out to the hurting, impoverished children by spending three days with them sharing the love of Jesus Christ.

I did not notice Ivan right away. Instead, on the first day, I saw the little girl with the faded blue and red ribbons on her dress sitting by herself, and I saw little Diego who could throw a Frisbee even though he was only 3. Out of the confusion of over 100 children playing, Dwain, one of our sponsors, approached me with four 9-year-old boys tagging along. They were asking for regalas, gifts, meaning that they wanted "Eternity Bracelets." These were bead bracelets each member of our choir made to give to the children as an explanation of the salvation Jesus offers us. While I retrieved my bracelets from the bus, Dwain led Ivan, Eduardo, Cristiano and Marcos away from the ruckus, and we all sat down beyond the bus so I could explain what the colors of the beads meant.

The boys listened, some more attentively than others, while I decoded the colors: black represents sin; red stands for Jesus' blood; white is the purification He brings; blue means baptism, a sign of one's decision to follow Christ; green is the growth of one's relationship with Christ; and gold reminds believers they will go to heaven when they die. Dwain had me ask the boys if they understood everything and wanted to let Jesus enter their hearts. "Si, lo quiero," they said. I led them in prayer to the Holy Father, "Santo Padre, quiero recibir a Jesus en mi corazon." "Santo Padre, quiero recibir a Jesus en mi corazon," they repeated in better Spanish than I had used. I will never forget how God used me to benefit the eternal future of those young boys.

On the second or third day of our Backyard Bible Club, Ivan brought me some children who did not have bracelets. I gave them bracelets but did not have to explain the colors because Ivan stayed to share what he knew about Jesus. Ivan's enthusiasm was contagious. Instead of worrying about being teased while jumping rope, his new-found, eternal perspective was evident as he shared the story of Jesus with his friends.

Why This Essay Succeeded

Some students are afraid to write about religion since they worry the reader may be of a different faith—or may have no faith at all. Admission officers are professionals and while each has his or her own personal views about religion, none would deny that religion can be an important influence. Religion is, therefore, a perfectly acceptable topic. However, what admission officers do not like is an essay that is preachy. You are not trying to convert them or convince them of the superiority of your religion over others. Nobody wants to be told what to believe. But as long as you stay away from this pitfall you can write a perfectly good essay about your religious faith.

In this essay, Michelle presents a nice vignette of the Backyard Bible Club. After reading her essay, the admission officers could probably envision the chaos of the children playing, the small group huddled around Michelle to learn the significance of the bracelets and her satisfaction from knowing that she has helped them. But notice that she is neither preachy nor judgmental about her religion. Instead, she describes her involvement as she would any other important extracurricular activity. She is selective about what she writes about and takes the time to dissect this single experience rather than attempt to cover her entire experience with the church. This ability to focus is important for any essay regardless of topic.

Lindsay Hyde

Miami, Florida

It takes a lot of courage for a high school student to pitch an idea to a top executive of a multi-billion dollar company. But this is exactly what Lindsay did, requesting funding from a vice president of Burger King for the Organ Donor Project she started. Her bravery was rewarded. She received the donation and then wrote and produced an informational video and educational curriculum to teach students at 12 U.S. schools and five international schools about organ donation. The graduate of Southwest Miami High School won numerous awards for her volunteerism, including the JC Penney Youth Volunteerism Award, National Coca-Cola Scholar award and Seventeen Magazine Youth Volunteer Award.

Organ Donor Project
Harvard University

It was still dark when I arrived early that morning at the Doral Golf Resort for the Pro-Am division of the Doral-Ryder Open golf tournament. As a member of the newly formed Southwest Miami High School girl's golf team, I had been presented with the opportunity to volunteer as a caddy at the tournament.

After checking in at the caddy shack, each volunteer was assigned a number and placed on a list. As the golfers arrived requesting caddies, the numbers would be called and the caddies assigned.

Finally, my number was announced. I reported to the check-in station and found that I had been assigned to Jim Watkins, a tall, well-dressed man carrying a seemingly enormous leather golf bag with a red and yellow Burger King logo emblazoned on the front. When I finally built up the nerve to lift the bag, I was as surprised as he that I was able to shoulder it. The 18-hole, four-hour walk had seemed menacing before. Now, with the weight of drivers, putters, wedges and irons teetering on my shoulder, the Blue Monster seemed ready to swallow me whole.

During the tournament Mr. Watkins questioned me about school and my involvement in extracurricular activities. He was particularly interested in the community service project I founded and coordinated, The Organ

Donor Project. As the day continued, I explained my motivation for creating the project, describing my grandmother's dual corneal transplant and my belief in the need for more accurate, teen-oriented organ donation information. I spoke about the three-day organ donation education event that I was in the process of planning and the tremendous outpouring of community support the Project already had received.

As we approached the 18th hole, the weight of the bag burning into my shoulder, the hot Florida summertime sun searing my cheeks, an idea began to form. From the very beginning of the Organ Donor Project, I had wanted to create an informational video that could be used within middle and high schools to dispel common teenage myths and misconceptions surrounding organ donation. Perhaps, I thought to myself as each member of the golf foursome putted his way to the end of the tournament, Burger King Corporation would be willing to sponsor the creation of such a video.

Walking off the course and back toward the caddy shack I was sure this was a risk worth taking. I held my head as high as I could, while crouching under the gargantuan bag, and looked straight ahead with confidence. I was going to ask him about my idea, and I knew without a doubt he would be ready and willing to move forward with my plan.

This confidence, however, quickly faded when we finally arrived at the caddy shack and my golfing partner was preparing to leave. I was no longer at all sure that this man with the painfully heavy golf clubs whom I had known for only four hours would be willing to listen to the fanciful ideas of a 16-year-old girl. Nerves had set in. But, as he turned to leave, I had the poignant realization that if I did not take this chance I would be tormented with thoughts of what might have happened and what I could have done. Clearing my throat, I stepped forward and began to speak.

As quickly as I could, I outlined my idea for the informational video and asked whether it would be possible for him to put me in contact with an individual at Burger King who would be able to authorize such a project. Using an undersized golf pencil, given to him to keep score during his game, he scribbled his name and contact information on a small slip of paper.

"Why don't you put together a proposal on your video and fax it to me. I'll take a look at it," he said and then strode into the resort. I could hardly believe what I had heard and quickly looked down at the makeshift business card to be sure. There it said, "Burger King, Vice President."

Nearly one year to the day later I received 250 copies of what became The Organ Donor Project "Fact or Fiction" video.

It amazes me how profoundly that one risk impacted my life. As a result of only 60 seconds of adrenaline and heart-pounding excitement, I have had experiences I may have never had access to otherwise. Though the actual completion of the video took only one year, the knowledge and skills I have gained as a result will last me a lifetime.

That morning it seemed as though the massive bag and the monstrous course were prepared to crush me. Instead, I emerged from the day only tired, slightly sunburned and completely elated. As a result, I realized the importance of stepping up, digging deep and taking the risks that may truly make a difference.

Why This Essay Succeeded

By receiving corporate sponsorship and creating an educational curriculum adopted by a dozen schools, Lindsay accomplished something that is quite extraordinary. If you have an amazing accomplishment like this you should definitely use your essay to highlight it. Imagine if Lindsay just listed the Organ Donor Project on her application and wrote about her love of tennis.

When it comes to impressive accomplishments, the essay is the best place to give the admission officers insight into what you have done. But even though Lindsay's accomplishment is impressive, she does not turn her essay into a brag session and neither should you. She uses her essay to explain what she has done and some of the risks that she took to do so. Whether you have accomplished something on a national level or neighborhood level, it's important to convey the significance in your essay. What challenges did you need to overcome? How were you motivated? What is the impact of your efforts? Let the facts and your work speak for themselves.

Alyssa Hochman

Virginia Beach, Virginia

A typical day for Alyssa began before 4 a.m., when she would rise to make it to the pool for swim practice. Her motivation for rising soon after other students went to bed? Simply put, she loves swimming, and in this essay, she explains her love. At Cape Henry Collegiate School, she also participated in student government. About writing her essay, she says, "I took personal events from my life and portrayed myself through the stories."

The Morning Ritual
Dartmouth College

Bewildered, I wake to the deafening sound of the latest pop song playing on my alarm-clock radio. I have learned that this is the only way to wake up at 3:57 in the morning. Quickly, I feel for the oval-shaped button, ending the music that I am sure will wake up my sister, fast asleep in the next room. I go through my early-morning ritual and quietly creep down the stairs, aided by the light of the moon. I grab my bag, packed the night before, and quietly shut the door behind me. I step outside and breathe in the salty morning air. I turn the key in the ignition, knowing that this is my last chance to run back to the comfort of my bed. Instead, I carefully drive the 21 miles to practice, forcing myself to keep my eyes open. The parking lot contains the cars of my fellow teammates. I pull in and am relieved to see that my coach has not yet arrived. I can enjoy a few precious minutes of sleep. Every morning we take part in the same unspoken ritual: arriving to practice early and sleeping in the warmth of our cars. The headlights of a small red car shine on my face as it pulls into the parking lot—the sign that my day has truly begun.

I walk onto the pool deck. The lights are just beginning to come on and the water is still. The powerful yet comforting smell of chlorine fills the air. Wearing our pajamas and parkas, we sleepily walk into our respective locker rooms. The floor is cold against my bare feet. I pull on my size 28 swimsuit—the same size suit I wore when I was 10. It is not that I haven't grown since then—quite the contrary; I am now 5 foot 10. A swimmer's body becomes accustomed to the tight lycra, which has now become my second skin. I step out onto the silent pool deck, water bottle in hand, and tell myself I can conquer any challenge my coach has contrived. He loves to try and defeat us mentally before we even take a stroke in the water, but I do not let him have that satisfaction. My cap is on, my goggles are tight, as I dive into the pool, breaking the calmness of the water.

One of my best friends wrote in my yearbook, "I can't believe you get up at 4 in the morning to swim. You're a nut." I am often asked why I swim. My answer is simple. I swim because I love it; it is who I am. I love being faced with a challenge and enjoy the satisfaction I feel when I have conquered my goal. Perhaps my friend is right. Maybe I am "a nut," but I am not alone; I have my teammates. When I enter the pool deck, I enter a place where I am content and fulfilled. There is no need to explain why I am at practice; my teammates and I share a bond, an understanding. It takes hard work and dedication, but as Jimmy Dugon said in *A League of Their Own*, "It's supposed to be hard. If it wasn't hard, everyone would do it. The hard is what makes it great."

Why This Essay Succeeded

Alyssa answers one of the most important questions that admission officers ask when reading any essay: "Why?" Why would she wake up at such an ungodly hour to swim? Why is swimming so important to her? By describing her morning ritual, the admission officers begin to understand the value of early-morning camaraderie, the dread and excitement felt at the first sight of her coach and the satisfaction of having accomplished so much before most other students have even awoken.

Obviously, Alyssa could have written about actual swim competitions or medals that she has won. But this would not be original. Think of the thousands of other athletes applying to college who will be writing about the "big game" and how after courageous effort they overcame the odds and won. Instead, Alyssa focuses on something far more important and significant, her motivation for swimming. We learn much more about Alyssa as a person (and are totally impressed by her commitment) than if she had just described which races she won. And even if we would not do so ourselves we can certainly understand why she gets up so early in the morning.

Shashank Bengali

Cerritos, California

Shashank is the kind of person who is not afraid of standing out. So even though most of his classmates did not join the Boy Scouts, he did. Through the organization, he learned valuable lessons not only about conquering the outdoors but also about looking inside himself. At Whitney High School, Shashank was the editor of the newspaper, student mentoring program volunteer and president of the Indian student organization. He won the Knight Ridder Minority Journalism Scholarship and Trustee Scholarship, providing a full tuition scholarship to attend USC.

The Gang
University of Southern California

I'm in a gang.

We're not a small group; this gang spans the entire nation, with offshoots in 116 countries around the world. The members of my gang are devoted and live their lives based on a code of conduct to which they are forever sworn. We will never all meet, but we all share the same beliefs and ideals.

The members of this brotherhood have faced ignorant peers. We are told that our gang is just a club of immature boys whose members are weak and frail. Despite our proficiency with knives and clubs, our honed survival skills and our keen practical knowledge, we are told we can't hold our own. Our structured lifestyle is labeled outmoded and impractical. We are the butt of jokes and taunts, of stares and pointing fingers, of relentless questions and unsatisfactory answers. Life is difficult but immeasurably rewarding.

We've been told to get out, to leave this gang and find a new set of friends and a new way of life. For all but a few, this pressure is too much to endure.

In six years worth a lifetime, the Boy Scouts of America has shaped my personal dogma. I have learned the value of friendship, truth, community and adherence to a moral code that I have found to be second to none. Scouts are partners in a personal stand against the general dumbing-down of moral values. "Sanctimony!" is often cried, but in truth, the fundamental tenets of truth and honor are perennially evident, and charity is never far from the hearts of members.

Cold winter mornings serving breakfast to the homeless, hot summer days repairing mountain trails in the Sierra Nevada and many an evening volunteering at local hospitals and churches have imparted to me a feeling of community, which I now fulfill as a volunteer at the local senior citizens center. Service has become an integral part of my life, and I feel greater compassion for those less fortunate, blessed as I am with such a rich environment in which to mature. I derived pleasure from working with mentally handicapped adults at the Association for Retarded Citizens and from organizing a charity drive for tenants of a local halfway house. Community service has helped me see life through different perspectives.

I have learned about leadership. I supervised 31 volunteers in the renovation of a park picnic shelter, a project I had designed myself. I was very gratified with the success of the job, but surprisingly, much more valuable than the praise I received was the heightened sense of confidence I developed. I was driven to seek more leadership roles to employ the practical skills I learned as a Boy Scout. Serving at the helm of two major campus organizations, the school newspaper and the Indian Club, could not have been possible for me had I not been somewhat seasoned as a leader and as a person. I came into these positions knowing how to deal effectively with people, how to manage crisis situations and how to work within a system to achieve the goals of an organization. I know what is required of a leader. In the past, I might have shrugged off my duties in positions of authority and thought nothing of it; now, I take my responsibilities seriously, often to the extent that they consume me.

Who I am today, the actions I take and the decisions I make all stem, whole or part, from what I have learned as a Boy Scout. Of course, I enjoy the camping, hiking and rock climbing and I am proud to be called an Eagle Scout, but these are finite destinations in a longer journey, and they pale in comparison to the lessons and the richness of the trip. I began as a wide-eyed 12-year-old, both ingenuous and insensitive about the world at large. Now I am poised to enter college, confident, equipped with real-world experiences and ready to take on new challenges. Such are the perks of life in this gang.

Why This Essay Succeeded

Writing about a common extracurricular club like the Boy Scouts requires a lot of extra planning. Shashank needed to approach his involvement in a way that other students would not. He accomplishes this by using a creative introduction that grabs attention and piques interest. That done, he presents his scouting experience in a way that distinguishes him from other scout applicants. He does this by focusing on specifics. Sure, many scouts will write about learning how to be trustworthy, loyal and kind but few will take the time to focus on the details and go beyond the what they learn and try to explain why it's important to them. Notice how Shashank provides explanations for what he gets out of community service and leading others. Even if the admission officers read 100 essays on scouting, Shashank's essay would still stand out.

Jeff Bozman

Hampton Roads, Virginia

Jeff might have taken it as a bad omen when he lost his voice the day of his Princeton interview. But with a good-spirited interviewer who supplied him with mugs of soothing hot chocolate, he successfully made it through. He says that the inspiration for his application essay came from the dean of admission, who advised him to focus on the essay. A graduate of Norfolk Collegiate School, Jeff participated in swimming, wrote for the school newspaper and became a National Merit Scholar. He would like to work in diplomacy or international business.

The 20 Other Points
Princeton University

"He got a 1580, but he's the dumbest kid I know." "Thanks, Steve," I reply. Steve is my swim coach, and he decided to use this comment to break the ice at a 5:30 a.m. swim practice in Raleigh, North Carolina. Or maybe it was Goldsboro? Or Chapel Hill? I can't remember. He was introducing me—complete with my dubious superlative—to the coach of a swim team with whom we were training. Our team was in the middle of a week-long "training trip," Steve's euphemistic term for dragging 30 swimmers across the state on a pool-hopping death march. We averaged five miles at each of our three practices per day. There were no breaks, no recovery periods and no easy practices. To an outsider, we must seem psychotic to get wrapped up in this cultish little ritual. We are. But nevertheless we are human beings and we needed something to get us through that week of Hell. Eventually I began to realize that my position as "village idiot" might give me both the opportunity to learn some lessons about human nature and the ability to help my teammates through some very trying times.

After I received my SAT scores a few weeks before, I had tried to tell the smallest number of people as possible. I've always been humble about my successes, and something of this magnitude would probably draw more resentment than admiration from my peers. So when Steve asked me how I did, I told him privately. He was proud, but as I was walking away, he asked (shouted, actually), "WHAT HAPPENED TO THE OTHER 20 POINTS?" Some of the replies that followed were: "What 20 points?" "What's he talking about?" "You mean you got an 80 on a test?!" After my explanations, I made a decision. I would transform myself into a harmless, clueless idiot savant and make the SATs look like a fluke. Following the examples of Lucille Ball and Art Carney, I gradually started to ask ditzy questions, trip and fall in the pool and don the infamous "deer in the headlights" look when things became complicated. Eventually my acting began to take hold; my stupidity never failed to break tension and the 1580 became a joke rather than a grade.

The training trip provided a unique opportunity to put my act to good use. Since he conceived of the idea, Steve has always fashioned the trip to be as much a test of emotional mettle as one of physical endurance. It always takes place in the few days right after Christmas, so the frigid (yet somehow never snowy) weather and even more frigid temperaments can play symphonic havoc with our emotions. By the end of the second day, I recognized that mood swings, bickering and short tempers were already starting to affect everyone's ability to perform; no one wanted to climb out from under their blankets and parkas to go swim, and consequently the swims were miserable, clock-watching marathons. So I began the sideshow entertainment. Eventually the collective mood began to brighten, people started to laugh and the last leg of the trip turned out to be one of the most hysterically happy moments of the entire week. Were we slap-happy? Probably. But no one there would ever deny the positive influence of laughter both on our swimming and on our relationships.

The training trip wasn't just a bunch of practices, nor was it an experiment in behavioral psychology. It was a blessing in disguise that taught me a great deal about myself. I learned that laughter is one of the best ways to defuse conflict and that I'm willing to generate it even at my own expense. Had I not, I never would have created my slapstick alter-ego, and the training trip probably would have resulted in one or two suicides. So you may very well laugh at me, thinking I'm "the dumbest kid you've ever met," but rest assured I'm laughing along with you. I'm bright enough to know what I'm doing; I DID get a 1580, after all! But let's keep that information quiet—I don't want to seem like a braggart.

Why This Essay Succeeded

Jeff does many things in this essay. First, he is not ashamed to admit that he plays the "village idiot" on his swim team. This ability to be self-deprecating is an admirable quality and displays a certain level of self-awareness and self-confidence. Next, Jeff makes us privy to a secret: this perception people have of him is based on a deliberate act. He is really exposing his inner self to us–total strangers. Third, Jeff includes concise examples and descriptions to show us how this "act" helped to transform what may have been an unhappy experience into one no one will ever forget. Our overall impression of Jeff is that he is a brilliant young man who understands himself and the psychology of his teammates–which of course is exactly what Jeff hopes we see.

Even though Jeff's essay is ostensibly about his involvement with swimming it really is a thoughtful portrait of his own psychology and intellect. Again, this is always the underlying purpose of the admission essay–to share with the colleges a slice of your life and to let them know who you are beyond your grades and test scores.

Memorable Essay: My New Brother
Director of admissions, Gettysburg College

"Each year there are essays that are shared in the office," says Gail Sweezey, director of admissions at Gettysburg College. The essays that seem to impress the Gettysburg College admission office most are those written from the heart. They present honest images of the writers and their feelings.

One essay that Sweezey recalls was about when the writer was 14 years old and her mother had another child. "That event completely changed her life. She did a wonderful job of capturing what her life was like at home and how this event had changed it. It was clear from her essay how thoughtful and responsible she was. It was a personal essay that really worked for her," says Sweezey.

Your passion and feelings when writing on a subject that you truly care about will naturally show through in your essay. Use this fact when picking a topic to make sure that your choice helps you write a better essay.

Essays About Music

Gregory James Yee

Cerritos, California

Gregory's music career began after his parents realized that without having taken a single music lesson, he could hum *The Star-Spangled Banner* in perfect pitch and rhythm–at age 2. Fifteen years later, the piano lessons he started while still a toddler paid off. The Whitney High School graduate has won numerous piano awards including the Raissa Tselentis Award given to one student nationwide for outstanding performance in the Advanced Bach category in the National Guild Audition. In addition to music, Gregory was a National Merit Commended Scholar, played on his school's varsity baseball team and is an avid sports fan, having collected the autographs of over 400 collegiate and professional athletes. While he wrote this essay for USC, he was also accepted to Stanford University.

How Rocky Changed My Life
University of Southern California

In fifth grade, my teacher asked the class to list our heroes. My friends repeated familiar names like Michael Jordan, Tom Cruise and Michael Jackson. My answer? Bill Conti. Who? You may not know his name, but you've certainly heard his work: the theme song to the movie "Rocky." Bill Conti is a musician, composer and, to me, hero.

I first saw him at a concert when I was 9 that featured several of his original compositions. The most stirring and inspiring that night was the "Rocky" theme. As the trumpet fanfare began the audience instantly recognized the music and erupted. For an unassuming man, he commanded the audience's undivided attention throughout the performance. That night I decided to become a composer.

When the orchestra performed the "Rocky" theme with Mr. Conti at the helm, it was the first time I had ever seen a man lead 80 other people performing a composition of his very own. He was like a painter who had an image in his mind and was conducting his understudies to create a majestic portrait before our very eyes. Unlike at any concert I had been to before, I wasn't listening to the notes written by someone centuries ago. From his own imagination, Mr. Conti created every note his orchestra played. Just as every ear-pleasing chord and flowing melody created a powerful image of Rocky preparing for a big fight, my music, like Mr. Conti's, expresses images and feelings in my mind.

Since that concert, I have written several award-winning compositions that I have performed on numerous occasions, including my sister's wedding and at the Cerritos Center for the Performing Arts. Last year I was honored by my high school band when they played one of my compositions. The concert by Mr. Conti inspired me to convey my feelings and emotions in the form of musical composition. My dream is to be an artist, writing music for the world to hear and conveying my thoughts through music.

Why This Essay Succeeded

There's something inspiring about witnessing a person's realization that they have discovered what they would like to do for the rest of their life. That's exactly what Gregory allows the admission officers to be a part of in his essay. In describing Bill Conti's concert, he shares what he heard and how he became inspired. Even someone who is not a music aficionado can relate to Gregory. In his story, it is not the subject that stands out so much as the verbs and adjectives.

Many people embrace music, perhaps you among them. Like Gregory did, make your story unique by making it intensely your own, and you will have written a winning essay. While Gregory could have focused on his own original compositions or performances, he chooses to emphasize something that is totally his own—how he fell in love with music. This is a unique topic that will not be shared with another applicant.

Andrew Koehler

Oreland, Pennsylvania

Andrew's love of music began at the age of 5 when he started playing the violin. While a student at Upper Dublin Public High School, he began playing in the Philadelphia Youth Orchestra, eventually becoming that orchestra's concertmaster. In this essay Andrew describes the orchestral Prelude and Liebestod from Wagner's opera "Tristan and Isolde." The essay's sentence structure and lack of paragraphs are intentional efforts to more closely mirror the music described. In addition to his contributions in music, Andrew founded the German Club at his school and speaks both German and Ukrainian. He plans to pursue a career in conducting.

Prelude and Liebestod
Yale University

The thin white baton is suspended for only a moment above the conductor's head. As it falls silently to its original chest-height position, the low strings begin their first hushed sounds. This is anguished music, full of tension. Again and again the same unsettling sonority appears, each time in desperate need of a resolution that is consistently and tortuously evaded. The music's protagonist is fatally injured; his pain becomes ever more acute, and the imminence of his death is unquestionable. He nevertheless fights to stay alive—not for himself, but for his one true love. Thick, dense chromatic scales in the upper strings, which repeat in succession, build to a moment of frantic intensity as the hero desperately tries to tear off his bandages so that his true love might never know the extent of his fatal injuries. This passionate gesture only worsens his condition, and two low notes in the double basses, played with great weight, signal the hero's inevitable death. With a haunting melody beginning in the woodwinds, the heroine approaches her lover. Realizing that he is dead, she begins to sing of her grief. Her song, passed delicately among the instruments of the orchestra, begins as a whisper. As the grief grows, so too does the tension in the musical texture, with each section of the orchestra eventually joining the collective in the singing of this song of tragedy. The music grows louder and louder still, and the passion reflected in the remembrance of this love becomes almost unbearable, until a point of saturation where it seems no longer possible to continue with such heart-wrenching pain, and it is at this point that the entire work's tremendous climax occurs, when all members of the orchestra play with full force and unspeakable intensity, an intensity which describes the death of the heroine, for she, too, has died, from the insurmountable grief caused by her lover's passing. Death hangs heavily in the air and the weary arpeggios in the strings begin to calm the music's atmosphere. With the finality of the last chord, the cloud of tension which had so long held throughout the work finally resolves. There can be no more grief, and the tragedy of two deaths lies cradled in the complete tranquility for which the music had fought so long to reach. Slowly, ever so carefully, the various players of the orchestra begin to sit back in their respective seats and put their instruments down, exhausted by the sublime power of music.

Why This Essay Succeeded

Andrew does not write about himself directly in his essay, but the admission officers still learn a lot about who he is. It's apparent that he is avid about music and has a level of understanding that few of us will ever possess. The way Andrew describes the music and his choice of words reveals his ability to hear and interpret music in a way that only a true musician can. Even if you have never heard this piece you can still imagine what it sounds like just by reading the descriptions Andrew provides. In an indirect yet unmistakable way, he shares a side of him that's real music to the admission officers' ears.

Sarah Medrek

Hammondsport, New York

Sarah has such close ties to music that she can almost hear her piano and trombone beckoning. In her essay, she describes her relationship with Wurly, the name that she has given to her piano. A graduate of Hammondsport Central School, she was the first chair trombone in the New York All State Symphonic Band, received a first place award in Fletcher's Piano Competition and attended the New York State Summer School of the Arts School of Orchestral Studies. She was also a National Merit Scholar and recipient of the Bausch and Lomb Science Award. She plans to work in engineering.

Wurly
Princeton University

Although it is 11:18 at night, I hear my piano, affectionately known as Wurly, calling me. From across the room he entices me with his white and black 88-toothed smile. He murmurs that my sheets of ragtime music and my collection of rock 'n' roll songs long to be read but instead lie dormant in his bench, soundlessly accumulating dust. I try to explain, "Wurly, it's 11:18 at night, and you can't wake up my parents. Tomorrow brings new opportunities." Like any recalcitrant child, he does not understand. He sullenly closes his lid to rest for the night.

No matter how often I tickle his smooth and polished keys, it is not enough. Neither my daily morning renditions of "Twist and Shout" nor my hour sessions in the afternoon with Bach, Chopin and Schumann suffice. I do not like to mention it, but Wurly is downright jealous of my liaisons with the piano at school, where I accompany the junior high chorus. I wish I could be mad with him and reprimand him for his insolence, but I cannot. I know he is right. He hates wrong notes: I play too many for his tastes. Wurly only wants the best and gets very jealous when I tell him of the flawless performance of Mozart's Sonata in G Major I heard while at orchestra rehearsal. I neglect to tell him that a 13-year-old kid played this, but somehow he knows and shames me into another few minutes plunking out the rhythm to Gershwin's Prelude #3.

If only I had unlimited time to play piano, I think wishfully. Not only would I satisfy the insatiable needs of Wurly the drill sergeant, I would bring myself contentment. Number Three on my list of lifetime goals is to become a virtuoso on the piano, able to play any piece of music thrown my way as if it were a one-finger version of Mary Had a Little Lamb. Although I come a sixteenth note closer to this goal every day, it is a slow process. It would take unlimited time and resources for me to be as good as I want to be.

The other items on my lifetime list of goals are more attainable. Someday, I will run a marathon; I just need to keep on jogging five times a week. Someday, I will speak Spanish fluently, as long as I continue to study Spanish and learn new words. Someday, I will be an unbelievably good trombonist; all I need to do is practice every day. These goals are a cinch compared to becoming a virtuoso piano player. They only require vigilant attention; perfect piano playing requires unthinkable amounts of time and an unfathomable amount of skill.

Why This Essay Succeeded

Sarah employs a creative approach by animating her piano and re-vealing her feelings about music and practice through her interaction with it. She also subtly weaves in her other life goals. After reading her essay, the admission officers understand how she feels about playing musical instruments, the importance they play in her life and how she motivates herself to achieve personal goals.

We all have idiosyncrasies that make us who we are. In this case Sarah has named and speaks to her piano. Some might call that crazy but to an admission officer it's a sign of honesty. After all, it is these quirks that make each of us unique. You should not be afraid to share yours in your essay.

Math and Science

Svati Singla

11-Year-Old Scientist
Duke University

While most of my friends were taking great interest in playing tag and kickball, I, as an 11-year-old child, needed something far more complicated to grasp my interests. My quest for knowledge seemed truly insatiable and I needed a unique avenue of learning. The idea of conducting professional medical research intrigued me; though I was only 11 years old, I was determined not to let my age hinder my extreme ambition and interest in higher level research. Thus, I picked up the phone book and began contacting labs in the East Carolina School of Medicine.

After a long stream of rejections and disappointment, I was finally acknowledged. The head of the Nuclear Cardiology Department recognized my genuine interest and scientific aptitude and invited me into his lab for an introduction of scientific principles and procedures. Though he was initially amused at the idea of such a young child conducting voluntary research in his laboratory, he presented me with various research options and I began a detailed study on the effects of elevated blood pressure on coronary heart disease.

I spent long hours in the lab searching through detailed medical histories and performing various tests on computerized images of the heart. After many months of tireless research, I finally came upon some astounding conclusions, and the findings of my research were published in the *American Journal of Hypertension*.

This publication marked a milestone in my life, a milestone with a clear message: a lesson that age should never be a hindrance in the way of goals and dreams.

After the conclusion of this study, I continued my research interests by initiating an experimental study in the Department of Biochemistry. The study dealt with the effects of drug abuse during pregnancy and fetal alcohol syndrome. After presentations at several science competitions, where it earned special commendation from the U.S. Army and U.S. Navy, I was convinced that there was nothing my dedication and optimism could not conquer.

Why This Essay Succeeded

For an outstanding accomplishment like Svati's—conducting research at the age of 11—it makes sense that she would write an essay about it. Svati does a good job of explaining the challenges she faced to be able to conduct the research—convincing the academics that she was serious about the task and committing herself to working in the lab. But what separates Svati from other students who have worked in labs? The answer is: Results. Svati is able to point to her conclusions being published in a respected journal to prove that she was not just messing around with test tubes but was involved with serious research. When you are describing an accomplishment it always helps to be able to give examples of concrete achievements. You want to make sure that the admission officers know that you have made a meaningful contribution.

Scott Itano

Homedale, Idaho

According to Scott, he is the second student in Homedale High School's history to attend an Ivy League college. While in high school, he was student body president, a competitor in the state's science competition and volunteer for SMELLS (Students Making Everyone Less Likely to Smoke or Spit), a group sponsored by the American Cancer Society.

In the Field
Harvard University

Experiences are the building blocks of life. They provide the blueprints for how I think and act. They are the sources for emotions such as bliss, puppy dog love or devastation as in a soap opera storyline. One of my most treasured events occurred this past summer when I attended the Student Challenge Awards Program (SCAP) in the Sierra Nevada Mountains in California. I studied plant responses to climate changes in the Western United States with seven talented high school students, two undergraduate students and a professor from U.C. Santa Cruz.

The biological research I did in California fulfilled years of wondering how field biology works. I lived in an environment for two weeks where knowledge saturated everything. I learned a multitude of new concepts and ways of thinking, not to mention how wacky teenagers can become when they're sleep-deprived. (Tree hugging is just one example.) I developed friendships with extremely gifted people who shared my love for science and actually understood how I felt. Honestly, words do not justify the feelings I have for this experience since they are sensations more powerful than immense satisfaction and gratification.

I will be indebted forever to the Durfee Foundation (sponsors of SCAP) for exposing me to the real world. Reflecting on my time in California, I see it as a life-changing experience. Instead of satiating my appetite for knowledge, it has only stimulated my hunger for it. I now realize how much of the world is yet to be understood and, more importantly, to be discovered. I am more aware of the world around me and my role in it. Everyday people like me can make a difference.

I will treasure my experience in California. It's the kind of memory that sticks like a person's first kiss. My trip instilled knowledge, awareness and hope in me. Because of this single experience, I believe I am a better person. Experiences can be diamonds in the rough, unsuspecting and silent until someone discovers them. Not only do experiences provide memories to savor but lessons for living.

Why This Essay Succeeded

In a way, Scott's essay is a coming-of-age story, although in his case it takes place on an academic level. His experience exposed him to research in the field and awoke in him a desire for continuing to conduct research. The admission officers could probably tell from his writing just how excited he was by the opportunity. For an essay on an academic subject, if you have the space it can also help to describe the actual research. —the questions you pursued and the answers you found. These details help the admission officers see your intellectual curiosity.

Notice that Scott does not only focus on the hardcore academic lessons. He comments on the effect of sleep deprivation and some of the silliness of working in the forest. All of this helps to ground his essay and show the admission officers that he is not just a student scientist but also a young person with a sense of humor who observes his fellow students as much as he does his experiments.

Jonathan Bloom

Orchard Lake, Michigan

Jonathan is a gifted mathematician. During his summers he conducted research at Ohio State University and General Motors. In his essay, he shows his passion for the field and achievements that he made while still in high school. He says the goal of his essay was to get the admission office to share his application with the mathematics faculty to gain the department's support. In his spare time he volunteers, water skis and juggles torches, knives and clubs.

Number Theory and Vehicle Weight Distribution
Harvard University

Near the end of my junior year of high school, I had yet to decide whether to accept a summer internship at General Motors or to return to the Ross Young Scholars Program at Ohio State University. The previous summer at Ross, while fully immersed in number theory for eight weeks, I developed a burning hunger for the in-depth study of mathematics. I learned how to think scientifically and perform research independently. The founder of the program honored me with an invitation to return as a junior counselor. In this capacity, I would have studied combinatorics while engaged in the development of first-year attendees. The founder and other OSU professors repeatedly urged me to come back to Ohio State, and one faculty member actually suggested that, at General Motors, I might be nothing more than "Captain Xerox." By taking their advice, I would have revisited a safe and familiar academic experience. Instead, I took a risk and entered the corporate world.

My experience at GM could not have been more successful. Based on my background, I was placed in the Operations Research Department of the General Motors Truck Group. I conducted a study that identified the most efficient method for accurately approximating the vehicle weight distribution for their product lines. Ten weeks later, I had completed the project, documented the results and given five presentations to increasing levels of management. General Motors is now looking at ways to quickly implement my findings, which will result in the company saving millions of dollars.

As the only high school student, it was a privilege to be a contributing participant in a fully operational corporate workgroup. I worked comfortably alongside many talented individuals, half of whom had their doctoral degrees. Invested with responsibility, I managed my assignment from inception through completion. I also sharpened my oratory skills, presenting volumes of technical data in a clear and concise manner. This required reading a textbook on statistics and learning the fundamentals of Visual Basic for Applications.

By not traveling to Columbus, I was able to take two courses at Wayne State University, study and pass-out of Spanish IV at my high school and lay the groundwork for my next research project at the University of Michigan-Dearborn. Because I live on a lake, staying at home gave me the opportunity to enjoy boating, jet skiing, water skiing and wake boarding with my friends. I even took a little red Corvette, a company car, out for a spin on Interstate 75. This summer, therefore, provided me with both a tremendous sense of accomplishment as well as an opportunity for relaxation.

During the course of my young life, I have taken many risks by participating in academic and extracurricular activities that are beyond my years. The events of these past two summers have given me confidence that I would thrive in a strong academic and research-oriented environment. I believe that I would be a positive addition to the student body at Harvard College.

Why This Essay Succeeded

There is no question that Jonathan is smart. However, this essay also allows Jonathan to show that his abilities can have a practical application and that he can work with people outside of academia. While the first two-thirds of the essay outline his interest and accomplishments within the sciences, the last two paragraphs allow Jonathan to also convey another aspect of his personality. He is not just a science nerd. He enjoys water sports and foreign language and even taking a spin in a Corvette. This helps to round out our image of Jonathan and show a side that is probably not obvious by looking only at his application.

David Foxe

Sussex, Wisconsin

What began as a curiosity in a few architectural sites resulted in something much larger. Over the past five years, David has visited over 600 architectural landmarks in the Midwest and Northeast, exploring the works of those including Wright, Pei and Eero Saarinen. He did much of his research while a student at Hamilton High School, where he was a National Merit Scholar, Tandy Scholar and Wal-Mart Scholar. He has accomplished all of this in spite of having Lamellar Ichthyosis, a rare and energy-consuming skin condition. About his condition he says, "It has caused me to realize my limitations but also to strive with my best efforts." For his application to MIT, David was asked to write his own question and then answer it.

Aesthetics and Calculus
MIT

David's Question: Describe how such seemingly different subjects such as aesthetics and calculus can be integrated (pun intended) to exemplify a larger pattern of interrelated creative and applied thought. Include obscure but pertinent references to Heisenberg, conga drums, Maurice Ravel, the history of German Literature and Alden B. Dow when applicable.

A principal characteristic that exemplifies my essay is that the question is more important than the answer, especially when the question requires thinking outside the box.

This topic is based on my research presentation, The Aesthetics of Calculus 1, which I found extremely interesting as a discovery process. The mathematical analysis tools of calculus can be applied to the artistic elements of life including photography, visual art, architecture and music. The relations described by calculus functions are crucial to a true comprehension of photography, technical aspects that allow for enhanced artistic expression within the realm of light and optics, media which allow us to visualize and appreciate the realm of visual art.

Stimulating and intricate works of art can be created from the math topics of topology, fractal geometric regression (an example of which I discovered in a math contest problem) and general aesthetic proportion. Especially meaningful to me are the examples I analyzed in the field of architecture in which hyperbolic functions of structural caternaries, hyperbolic paraboloid concrete marvels and other unit-based geometric works by Alden B. Dow, F.L. Wright and Santiago Calatrava. Finally, I explored the mathematical descriptions of waves for musical instruments, such as organ pipe lengths and the volume of wood that allows percussive resonance in conga drums.

This independent research has helped me to clarify that I want to pursue an education that will allow me to enrich an understanding not only of scientific analysis, but also of the aesthetic creative development. This mathematical learning has caused me to enjoy such hobbies as photography and (almost concert-level) piano even more because I can appreciate the principles supporting them, such as the complex harmony of compositions by Maurice Ravel. I have learned that architecture best integrates many different elements of art, music, engineering, history and math to create a more efficient and beautiful environment to benefit the people who live and work with these buildings. Therefore, the intellectual environment of MIT best encompasses the knowledge to pragmatically accomplish the creative problem-solving for building people up through their architectural environment.

Why This Essay Succeeded

Good essays demonstrate how a student sees his or her fit with the college. Without beating you over the head, David shows his match with MIT. This college seeks students who are talented in fields like mathematics and who can relate their book learning to the real world. Wouldn't you agree David has demonstrated he is MIT material? We certainly believe the admission officers did.

Jobs and Careers

Jason Garber

Hutchinson, Kansas

A natural entrepreneur and computer whiz, Jason combined the two to start a computer-related business at the age of 14. Through his business, he has sold and serviced computer hardware and software, developed and hosted websites and provided computer training. At Hutchinson High School, Jason was also involved in the choir, band and as president of the National Honor Society. In writing his essay Jason went through many drafts. "I just kept tweaking, revising and having others read it for quality, content and clarity," he says.

More Than a Tutor
Eastern Mennonite University

Being known as a computer tutor for the elderly hasn't won me many dates—at least not with women under 60. It has, however, brought me in contact with a generation of people who have a lifetime of wisdom and experience to share.

I enjoy tutoring a great deal because it allows me to interact with individuals more personally than one managing his own business is typically able. Through it, I gain a window into their lives and the things that have shaped their personalities. One of my favorite examples of this is an 81-year-old widow who has determinately used her computer to enrich others' lives, despite the barriers her health puts forth.

Nearly every Saturday, at 10 o'clock, I arrive at her home. She welcomes me in, immediately beginning to tell me about the triumphs and tribulations of her week. On Monday, she went to the dentist, and now she can't seem to suck her milkshake through a straw. Then, on Wednesday, her dishwasher of 15 years went out and made a terrible mess all over the floor... Quite often, we can spend a half hour or more discussing the events of our respective lives.

After some time, our conversation segues into my excuse for visiting: tutoring her on the computer. She takes out a list of questions and tells me the things that she wants special help with as I sit down on the wicker bench beside her. We address each item—making greeting cards for sick friends, sending e-mail to her son, chatting with her sister in Wisconsin, searching for recipes on the Internet—but frequently digress whenever we want to share something amusing.

When she has absorbed as much as she cares to, she glances up at the clock and echoes the advice I gave to her after our first meeting. "Well, I'll play with it," she says, intending to spend some time in the next week trying out her newfound abilities.

Before I leave, she often needs a jar opened, a top shelf reached or a melon cut. As we progress toward the door, we continue talking, neither of us wanting to end our reunion. At last, I must tear myself away, and my grandma of sorts watches from the window as I drive away, already beginning to miss my company.

On my way home, I'm filled with thoughts of what her life was like when season Packers tickets cost $12, when she stood before the class and recited her arithmetic and when her late husband, the judge, found homes for orphans and did widows' taxes for a dollar. As I turn into my garage, I recognize with a smile that through our relationship, I've given her comfort and company and received a little more wisdom and understanding to tackle the challenges of the week ahead.

Why This Essay Succeeded

There's something heartwarming and memorable about Jason's essay, the way he takes the time to converse with, assist and perhaps most importantly, appreciate, this senior citizen widow. This essay helps Jason to set himself apart from other applicants by showing this detailed level of respect and compassion. On top of that, Jason has the maturity to appreciate and really take to heart what the senior shares with him. The admission officers can tell that he is the type of person who is very insightful and self-reflective. In any essay you want to present a few of your best personal qualities.

Meena Anand

Burr Ridge, Illinois

Meena's visits to the hospital with her father as a child had a strong impact on her. She has been a hospital volunteer and observer and is contemplating a career in medicine. In her essay, Meena writes about the influence medicine has had on her. At Hinsdale Central High School, she also planned numerous public service events as the president of the Key Club and played tennis as a state doubles champion and as a member of her high school's state champion team.

Visits to the Hospital
Princeton University

When I was a little girl, I used to go to the hospital with my dad. I would sit in the waiting room while he went into the operating room and worked his magic. After the operations, he would take me with him to talk to his patients. Their gratitude and hopeful faces made me proud of my dad. It made me want to be a doctor just like him and his dad. One could just pass this off as a childhood fantasy, but I could not be more serious. Throughout middle school and high school, science has always been my favorite subject. Finding out about how things work and the foundations for life intrigue me. At school, even in writing classes, I found medicine to be the subject of paper after paper, thus allowing me to satiate my thirst for knowledge in the field and getting a paper done for class at the same time. I also tried to take the highest levels of science courses. I want to know how one little mutated cell can cause an entire system to shut down with cancer and if a cure for AIDS can ever be found. But this will only come with a more thorough scientific education, which Princeton has to offer.

Over the summers of my high school years I volunteered at LaGrange Memorial Hospital. I wanted to get as much exposure to the hospital as possible. I started out at the family care and practices center and then moved on to the gift shop. Both these experiences allowed me to interact with patients and their relatives. The true test was to see if I would actually want to perform the magic that my dad did behind the solid, white doors. He allowed me to watch him scope a patient for an ulcer and I found his work to be very interesting. As a result of my keen interest and excellent academic performance, I was invited to attend the National Student Leadership Conference for Medicine at Washington, D.C. There I got a true taste of the nature of medical work. Not only did I get to see a video of a heart transplant, but I also got to attend numerous lectures about the history of medicine, organ transplants and research opportunities given by respected physicians. These experiences have strengthened my desire to go into the field of medicine.

My most important reason for wanting to be a doctor is because I care. I hate to see people suffer. I remember visiting one of my dad's patients in a recovery room. He was a very nice old man. As we walked away, I also remember my father telling me that he would die within a month, despite everything my dad had done for him. I felt pain and regret stir up within me. If I could, I would try and find a cure for every disease that brings pain to patients and their families and try to save everyone, but that is not possible. But I do know that I can work as hard as I can to operate on a patient and save his life. And I can run experiments in the lab and try to find a way to develop a remedy for an incurable disease. I would also try to prevent illnesses from consuming patients by taking preventive precautions and teaching them what they can do to maintain healthy lives. Each person is a precious individual, and I want to do my best to save each one that may come into the care of my hands. For me, it is important that "to the world I may be just one person, but to one person I may just be the world" (unknown).

Why This Essay Succeeded

Every year countless students write about how they want to become doctors, scientists, engineers or another dream profession. If you're one of them this year, set your essay apart from the others. Notice Meena's approach, which is focusing on why you are determined to enter a specific career field. In her essay, Meena shows us the genesis of her interest in medicine and why she feels so strongly about becoming a doctor.

Meena also does not resort to platitudes. Of course, everyone wants to help others and make a difference. But Meena provides examples of why she feels the way she does about medicine. She shares her experience volunteering at a hospital and what she's learned through the leadership conference. By describing her interaction with the patient, she's able to demonstrate why caring for a patient is important. Her use of examples makes her statement that she hates to see others suffer ring true and not hollow.

Essays About Issues

Lily Johnston

Federal Way, Washington

When a close friend attempted suicide, Lily reevaluated her priorities and had some realizations about the expectations placed on females. She volunteered with the Real Women Project, an organization that seeks to show the beauty of women. She says, "Writing about depression, body image and how this affects young women was a natural extension of my work at Real Women as well as my way of pulling together what I was experiencing personally with what I was observing publicly." At Charles Wright Academy, she was editor of the yearbook, a managing editor of the newspaper and captain of the volleyball team.

In for the Long Crawl
Princeton University

We died that day. Not her, not I, we. She came close enough for the both of us. I can still remember that feeling of the earth just dropping out from underneath me when my mom told me that Chris had tried to kill herself. The worst part was that I wasn't surprised. I knew she had been "sick" for years, but that old scar on her wrist was always "a scratch from the coffee table." Since that day, we have never shared a secret or dreamed up a new fantasy—the "we" that had defined us for so long, those 10 years of friendship, that sisterhood, was the one thing she swallowed that a stomach pump couldn't remove. From that day on, I made it my mission to find the cause of the nation-wide epidemic of depression that had shattered our lives and to do everything in my power to find a cure.

In her world, everything was warped. In her delusion, a pocketknife, a gift that should have marked her coming-of-age and responsibility, became the "coffee table." Her grandfather's illness, which should have been sad but a natural part of life and living, was seen only for the drugs it would provide her for death and dying. I watched as she dug her own grave for two years. I don't feel guilty; I did everything I could to help her but alert the newspapers. What I would later understand and what would fuel my desire to help others was that she couldn't process or even understand help at that point; she was too sick.

My family is the only reason I didn't share her fate, they are why she ended up in a mental ward and I didn't. They were the only substantial difference between Chris and me: we were both depressed, we both had few close friends and we both were too young for our grade and too old for our own good. It was the little things that really counted. My parents didn't yell at me or each other. My sister and I never fought. My father didn't commute to another state regularly. I felt sorry for Chris and her family, but I realized early on that I couldn't control people's families or home lives, so I changed my focus to the things that I saw around me that made people feel "less-than" and incomplete.

Opening my eyes has never been such a powerful experience. I began to see things all around me that had the potential to make people, especially girls, feel depressed. Around every street corner, in every shopping mall and even in museums these images and ideas accosted me: anorexic girls modeling the latest fashions and the latest fashions only available in sizes 0 to 10 are a few examples. At one point I wondered if there existed some large-scale conspiracy to make all the girls in the United States depressed. The idea of social, physical and intellectual perfection was defined and fed to us as if there were such a thing as perfection and it could be defined only one way. It was all of a sudden a wonder to me that we all didn't just start jumping off cliffs, one after another like lemmings.

Trying to reverse a nationally accepted image has been like trying to crawl up Mt. Everest. As one might expect, I've made little headway and have run into more obstacles than I can count. Apparently, it's common for people to be advocates for women but to be much stronger advocates for their own pocketbooks. "Yes, we would really like to promote reality," they say, "but people don't buy reality. We're a business, not a charity." But, for Chris' sake, and for the hope that our relationship may still be salvaged someday, I will keep crawling as long at it takes to save one life, for if I can save one life, I have saved two. If I have saved two, I've saved them all. If I've saved them all, I've finally saved myself.

Why This Essay Succeeded

One of the biggest mistakes that many students make when writing about an issue is that they do not personalize it. They write about an issue as they would for an assignment for a social studies class rather than for a creative writing class. Whatever the issue, there needs to be a reason why it is important to you. Clearly, teen depression is a huge national issue. But Lily does an excellent job of making it close to home. Her essay covers both her individual experience with depression and some of the larger societal issues that she believes perpetuate it.

Notice that her essay contains a lot of thoughtful reflection. She realizes that she can't change the world in one fell swoop but she also knows that there are things she can do to help. This essay is not so much a display of her writing ability as it is of her ability to think, feel and analyze.

Donald H. Matsuda, Jr.

Public and Private
Stanford University

Public or private, which is better? I began to ponder the social ramifications of the distinctions between life in the public sector and life in the private sector, having recently experienced both sides of the issue.

I can clearly recall my ambitions as first-year editor of my high school yearbook, an organization that I soon discovered was identical in process to the public sector. My prevalent suggestions on improving the efficiency of the Copy Design Department had to be thoroughly evaluated and approved by a large hierarchy of administrative individuals prior to even being considered by the moderator or fellow editors. Such a dilatory process evoked an understandable sense of frustration among several yearbook staff members, and many more felt the contravening effects of strictly imposed regulations.

My employment at a privately owned business provides a stark contrast to the editorial inhibitions and prescribed responsibilities of managing a high school publication. In this private sector enterprise, decisions must be made swiftly and efficiently in order to maximize the profit for the company. Thus, the workers are free to make their own corporate decisions; however, they must be willing to accept both the positive and negative consequences of their actions.

My experience has intrigued me to consider the more significant question: public or private, which is better for me? I strongly believe that both the public and private sectors have myriad opportunities to offer, and consequently my ambition of a career in the field of medicine will hopefully permit me to experience both sectors. This would not only be possible in a medical career, but it would also establish a most effective practice, a perfect balance between guidelines and freedoms. The regulations established and enforced by HMOs currently provide important guidelines for physicians to adhere to, while at the same time, a private practice gives them the flexibility to operate their business as they please. This vision gives me great hope for an exciting future career in the public and private sectors that uniquely combines the best of both worlds.

Why This Essay Succeeded

In tackling complex issues, it helps to simplify them and avoid writing in the abstract. Donald does this by providing concrete examples of his experience with the bureaucracy of the yearbook and the quick decision-making of the business world in the private sector. He further personalizes the essay by rephrasing the question from: "Which is better public or private?" to "Which is better for me?" This allows Donald to take a stand based on his own understanding of himself and which would fit his approach and style better. When it comes to large issues there is nothing wrong with reframing the question so that you can answer it on an individual level.

Anonymous

On Prejudice
Princeton University

Prejudice is not something that people are born with. In the argument of nature versus nurture, prejudice is the product of environment and experience. This year, one of my good friends passed on. She was a beautiful elderly Jewish lady whose experiences in life taught me a great deal. She is one of the nicest people I have ever met, and yet she did not like black people.

Most people think that prejudice is the result of ignorance and stupidity, but she was very well educated. The reason she hated black people was because almost 20 years ago, a black man that she had helped to find a job and a home beat her mercilessly and stole many of her precious belongings, including sight in one eye. From that one horrible experience, she closed the door on black people and refused to like them. No one can even begin to improve relations between races until people realize that someone's race does not account for their individual actions. The color of my skin does not make me any more prone to violence or intelligence. In the age of statistical accuracy, people are so used to making generalizations that they don't realize that it's not a matter of black, white, brown or yellow. Everyone is different and you cannot blame the actions of one on many.

There is this program in LA where gang members who want to improve their place in life bake bread. A local priest began the program. It is amazing because people who would have killed one another six months ago are now working side by side and even becoming friends.

My school is diverse in terms of racial background and there has always been some racial tension. A lot of my good friends think that there is no way to improve race relations because of those individual experiences I mentioned above. But I think that it is from those individual differences that improvement will spring. I think that if we can have individuals working together towards some common goal, to clean up a local elementary school or to bake bread, they will learn that there are good as well as bad people in every race.

We must not forget the children in our society either. Schools need to be diversified so that kids will be forced to interact with other kids of every race and learn on their own that the racism that their parents or friends feed them is not always the truth. Everyone needs to learn that it is the individual, not the race that he or she is categorized under, that makes them who they are.

Why This Essay Succeeded

An issue that is as complex as race relations can be difficult to tackle in the short space of a college admission essay. The key is to avoid being general and instead be specific. This writer gives the examples of the prejudiced senior citizen, the transformation that occurs in former gang members and the opinions of the diverse students at school. By using these examples, the issue of race becomes an individual one.

The writer also gives opinions on the problem and possible solutions. While these solutions are not designed to be matters of public policy, they are the type of individual actions that everyone can do to address the problem in their own small way. Nobody expects you to solve the world's problems in a 442-word essay. But the admission officers do expect you to be able to analyze the key issues, give examples from your own life and present the conclusions that you have arrived at in your own opinion.

Jeff Bozman

The Hawaiian Good Luck Sign
Princeton University

Of all the apparent junk mail that flows through my e-mailbox, one particular anecdote stands out as a very entertaining story. The tale of the Hawaiian Good Luck Sign highlights the importance of good communication. The story concerns a clueless woman who, while driving, accidentally cuts off another driver, who in turn flips her off. Not knowing what that means, she asks her street-savvy daughter. The girl tells her mother that it is the Hawaiian Good Luck Sign. "Oh," the woman thinks, "how nice of him!" She proceeds to give the Hawaiian Good Luck Sign to everyone she passes, and—how about that!—everyone gives it right back to her! About the same time, she spies a bumper sticker that reads: "Honk if you love Jesus." Since she was in such a good mood already, she decides to spread the Good News of Jesus with everyone else. All of the other cars must be on their way to a religious convention, she imagines, because all of them REALLY love Jesus! What a wonderful day!

While a bit farfetched, the story emphasizes the fact that communication (or miscommunication, as it were) is at the heart of every aspect of daily life. Thus, in order to prevent another disaster like the one above, I would invest my time and talents into a traveling study of languages. Not only would my language skills enable me to converse with people in their native tongue (one of the highest compliments one can pay a foreigner), but they would open up opportunities for a more comprehensive liberal arts education. So far, my studies have been extremely Western-focused. In part, I blame the Anglo-American arrogance associated with the prominence of our language for this egocentric approach to education. Gregg Cox, who holds the world record for speaking the most languages (64) says, "People are so surprised—not that I speak so many languages, but that I'm an American and I speak so many languages!" If I were able to read the teachings of Confucius, Buddha and Mohammed in their original contexts and converse with people who have lived all their lives with these philosophies, I would undoubtedly gain a more erudite perspective from which to evaluate the conflicts of our modern global society.

Why This Essay Succeeded

While this essay begins with a lighthearted story, it also introduces the core of Jeff's thesis: the importance of good communication. An "important issue" does not have to be one that headlines the evening news. You can do as Jeff has and pick a less-obvious topic. Notice, too, that Jeff ties in his own skills and goals of traveling and learning new languages. Like all of the essays in this section, Jeff is providing a solution to the problem that is very personal. It represents his contribution to improving the world's communication problem starting with himself.

Overcoming a Weakness or Challenge

Rita Hamad

Austin, Texas

What she lacks for in stature, Rita makes up for in determination. A world traveler, she writes about her shared height with Napoleon and her comparable drive. It is this resolve that enabled her to advance from English as a Second Language classes within a few months of immigrating to the United States in elementary school. She now speaks English, Arabic, Spanish and is learning Japanese. While a student at the Science Academy at LBJ High School, she was involved in the Latin Club, held an internship at the M.D. Anderson Cancer Center Research Division and became a National Merit Scholar. She plans a career in law or medicine.

All of 5'1"
Harvard University

As a freshman in world geography, our teacher showed us a documentary about Napoleon and his conquests of Europe and the Mediterranean region. Everyone oohed and ahhed when they heard of the general's domination of almost an entire continent. Admittedly, I too was somewhat impressed by the performance of the little man with his hand in his coat. A few minutes into the video, the narrator announced that Napoleon stood at a height of 5'1". As soon as the words were out of his mouth, the whole class turned around to look at me and giggle. When you're as short as I am, you can't help being noticed. Yet I was pleased in a way that I had something in common with such a great historic figure. I was sure that as Napoleon marched around the battle field in his doll-sized clothing, his soldiers laughed at his crackpot military ideas. He must have faced great obstacles on his road to fame and fortune. And as a 13-year-old minority female, I couldn't help but smile at the similarities.

When I first came to the United States to attend kindergarten, I was only 4 years old and still a little shaky in my English, so the elementary school I attended put me in English as a Second Language (ESL). I was only in the class for a few months, though, when my teachers realized that all I needed was a little confidence. Soon I was reading faster and at a higher level than all the children in the Aim High English classes. By the time I reached the first grade, I was making straight A's. But after the second grade, my family moved to Bahrain, a small island in the Arabian Gulf. There I had to relearn Arabic and deal with the cultural shock of returning to a Middle Eastern country. Even this situation didn't last very long, and I was back in Austin for sixth grade. At this point, I had learned to adapt to change very quickly, and the little girl who had taken ESL received first place in UIL Spelling in the Austin Independent School District as a seventh grader. Due to all of our traveling, however, I didn't know that there was a magnet school for junior high school until it was too late, so I didn't get the chance to display my full potential. In fact, my eighth grade algebra teacher tried to discourage me from challenging myself. She said that I should take my time in high school, take one math credit per year—especially if I planned to attend the Science Academy. Being as determined as I am, I rejected these notions and signed up for both Algebra II and Geometry as a freshman. Within a few months, I had proved her wrong. I quickly shot up to become valedictorian of my class, and two years later I made a 5 on the Calculus BC AP.

From that point on, nothing could stand in my way. If anybody told me I wasn't capable of achieving something, I took it as a challenge. Against the odds again, I ran for president of the Latin Club as a junior and succeeded. Over the summer I planned several carwashes and solicited corporations for contributions to fund the upcoming trip to Italy, an event that even the sponsor doubted I could pull off. But that spring, he was happy to see that I was successful. At the end of my term last year, the club presented me with an award that I now treasure more than any of the trophies I've received at the various competitions I've attended: "Most Likely to Take Over the World: to Rita Hamad, for her Napoleonic Complex... Short on Stature, Long on Ambition." They guessed it! Although I have no intentions of overthrowing the government, I do intend to conquer everything I set my mind to. In a sense, Napoleon will be one of my role models in school, in my career and for the rest of my life.

Why This Essay Succeeded

The essay can be an opportunity to provide context to your achievements with a level of detail that is just not possible through the application form itself. Rita does this by sharing with the admission officers the various challenges she needed to overcome. In addition, Rita reveals her sense of humor. Poking fun at her diminutive size, she contrasts it with her extraordinary determination. The admission officers probably appreciated her creative approach and the way that she carried the Napoleonic theme from start to finish. Providing additional background like Rita does helps the admission officers understand not only what you've done but also the conditions under which you did it.

Daniel Alexander Uribe

Houston, Texas

Not many students would voluntarily choose to make life more difficult for themselves, but this is exactly what Daniel did. Unchallenged by his high school, he transferred to YES College Preparatory High School for a more rigorous academic curriculum. At YES, he participated in student council and YES Family, in which he mentored younger students. He wrote this essay for the University of Miami but decided to attend Cornell University.

Bench-Pressing My Education
University of Miami

Saturday morning—I was determined to accomplish the task that lay before me. I was not only doing it for myself, but for all my friends who had tried but failed.

This morning, however, I believe the odds were on my side. The struggle began, and once again, I felt myself succumbing to its power; however, I was not going to go down without a fight. I felt that I was crushing the cold steel, bending and twisting it. With every squeeze of my palm, the cold sweat on my forehead slowly disappeared and I saw myself winning. I was finally doing it—I was bench-pressing 200 pounds!

To many people, bench-pressing 200 pounds may not be a significant achievement. For me, it was more than just the physical act. Before I accomplished this goal, I spent many hours in my backyard gym. At first, I failed to see the fruits of my labor because I wanted quick results. Disappointment set in, and I did not see myself improving. After I bench-pressed 200 pounds, I realized something beyond lifting the actual weight: success or rewards are not always going to be initially apparent. The hours of work in the gym, the sweat and the soreness all helped me understand the commitment and dedication needed to accomplish my long-term goals.

This same idea holds true with my education. At Milby High School, I felt that I was not being challenged academically, so I decided to transfer to YES College Preparatory, a school with a rigorous academic program.

At first I was overwhelmed with the amount of work. I resisted and resented what teachers asked of me; I did not see the advantages of doing it. I felt that I was back in the gym and once again, the hard work was not showing immediate results.

Consequently, I shut down mentally and refused to work because I truly felt my efforts were in vain. However, my overall attitude changed during my junior year as I began to embrace the challenge of proving to myself that I could handle the course load. My grades improved and I found myself thriving in this environment. The summer before my senior year, I had the opportunity to attend a challenging summer program at Stanford University focusing on philosophy. Besides learning about Plato's theories, I also realized during those three weeks that the work that I had done in school and the high level of expectations placed on me by my teachers helped prepare me to be a successful student in this program. This unique opportunity existed because of the hard work and commitment that I had finally shown in school, just as I had shown in the gym.

Reflecting on my first two years of high school, I, like so many others, wish that I could go back and redo them. However, I feel fortunate to have gained this insight when I did, for I know now that while I cannot change the past, I can always shape my future.

Why This Essay Succeeded

This essay may have been quite ordinary if not for the fact that Daniel deftly draws a parallel between weightlifting and learning. He is able to connect the two skills and show how his experience overcoming the 200-pound barrier also helped him excel in school. This is an attention-getting connection to make.

Daniel's essay also shows that he is not afraid of a challenge. But he is a realist and understands that achievements–both physical and mental–take time and dedication. Daniel does an excellent job taking an otherwise common topic and turning it into something uniquely his own while showcasing his strengths to the colleges.

Erica Laethem

Caro, Michigan

Erica overcame a speech impediment to become a theatrical performer and debater. She wrote about this challenge in her essay. She says, "I believe that those frustrating years helped mold me into the person I am today." At Caro High School, she was also the band drum major, homecoming queen and a varsity swimmer and soccer player. Erica plans to enter the field of medicine to help others overcome difficulties as she did.

A Personal Challenge
University of Michigan

"I am convinced that life is 10 percent what happens to me and 90 percent how I react to it," Charles Swindoll lectured in his famous speech entitled "Attitude." By overcoming a tormenting affliction, I have developed one of my most treasured gifts.

When I was in second grade, my teacher expressed concern about the way I stumbled on words in a conversation. At the beginning of the year, my stuttering was only a minor impairment, but by January, it had grown into a full-blown predicament. I was so difficult to understand that listeners would either interrupt me by telling me to "spit it out!" or they would simply tire from trying to comprehend my "foreign dialect" and give up conversing with me altogether. My teacher recommended that I see the speech therapist who visited the elementary school regularly. Each time I would leave the classroom for my session with the "therapist," a name that denoted "psychoanalyst" to my classmates, my farewell was addressed with young voices echoing my impediment, "Buh-buh-buh-bye, Erica!"

The mockery projected from the mouths of classmates was humiliating, but the pain incurred from an adult was even more agonizing. In the spring of my second grade year, Sister Loretta asked my Sunday school class if anyone was interested in reading a gospel selection for our congregation for our First Communion ceremony. When I eagerly raised my hand, my Sunday school teacher argued, "Oh, Sister, don't pick her...she stutters!" I felt ashamed and incompetent as my classmates nodded their heads to endorse my teacher's assertion. Sister kindly replied, "I think she'll do just fine."

On the way home in the car, I burst into tears. I was so hurt by my Sunday school teacher's discouragement that I wanted to resign from my newly appointed position. My mother, who was as upset as I, lifted my chin and said, "Well, I guess we'll just have to prove her wrong, won't we?" As soon as we returned home, I began practicing that reading. I practiced that single piece for at least 30 minutes a day, every single day. Soon, the repetition from solitary studying and speech therapy began to show results. On that First Communion Sunday, I spoke with clarity and enunciation, with enthusiasm and confidence. I had transformed my teacher's devastating statement into the motivation that powered my vigorous training of repetition.

My First Communion was only the beginning of a whole-hearted struggle to overcome my impediment. I continued to practice with the speech therapist and at home with my parents. The struggle was not brief, but the process improved my senses of perseverance and dedication. If I hadn't been faced with the challenge to surmount my speech impediment, I would have never developed the enthusiasm to excel in communication arts. In the seventh grade, I auditioned for our community theater's musical production of "The Secret Garden," and was cast as the leading role of Mary Lennox. The call informing me of my acceptance at the Thumb Area Center for the Arts confirmed that I really had won the battle. Overcoming my speech impediment has opened doors that never would have been opened if I hadn't been "blessed with that given 10 percent" to conquer.

I have been asked, "Erica, if you could change one part of your life what would it be?" Most people who knew me when I was younger assume that I would love to omit the part of my life when I was tormented because of my severe stuttering problem. I usually surprise them when I say, "I wouldn't change a thing." That time of my life taught me how to overcome life's adversities. Most importantly, it taught me the importance of encouragement, sensitivity and kindness.

I wish to extend the fulfillment of overcoming challenges with a University of Michigan education. The standard of academic excellence that the University provides will serve as a superior foundation to build my future upon. My dream is to pursue a career in medicine where my work will propel my patients to experience the joy of conquering adversity.

Why This Essay Succeeded

When writing about a challenge, it's best not to spend too much space describing it but to focus more on how you have overcome it. Erica explains her test, the torment she faced from classmates and the determination she had to ultimately triumph. Through her selection of examples, she doesn't trivialize her efforts but instead explains how much work it took. The essay is both uplifting and inspiring and speaks volumes about her determination and commitment.

Success does not have to be earth shattering—in Erica's case her first victory is simply reading a gospel without stuttering. But success of any magnitude is impressive if you overcome tough obstacles to achieve it. And admission officers respect that. Using your essay to explain how you overcame a difficulty—rather than describing the challenge itself—will make for a much more powerful essay.

Nenhan Zhang

San Mateo, California

Nenhan is the persistent type. When he immigrated to the United States, he mastered the language to become an outstanding student. In swimming, he progressed from most improved swimmer his sophomore year to most valuable his junior year to team captain his senior year. While a student at Burlingame High School, he also participated in the math club and volunteered at the Coyote Point Museum. After college he plans to become an architect.

From Struggle to Success
U.C. Berkeley

As I draw my red photo album from the bookcase, wiping away the thin layer of dust that has obscured its cover, I pause to heighten the anticipation. This album has been my treasure box, its covers storing memories of my childhood in my native China. Opening up my album, I see a photograph of my father. I hear his wise reminder on the key to success: "If you want to survive, you have to put in twice as much effort as anybody else."

Attending an American high school has added new images to my autobiography. The moment I walked into the English as a Second Language classroom of Burlingame High School, I saw what my father meant by "survival." I have a mental photograph of myself at that classroom doorway, stopped by the fear and turmoil within my mind, wondering what I would do if someone spoke to me. Would I use my limited English, or would I rely on hand gestures to get my point across?

I did, however, survive. I knew that giving into intimidation was useless; I had to confront this challenge to understand and to be understood by others. When I tired of flipping through my English-Chinese dictionary, reflecting on this goal reminded me how much I still needed to learn in order to catch up with the people who sat next to me in my classes, and I worked harder. At the end of my freshman year, my work earned me both a satisfying grade and an acceptance into the next level of College Prep English.

The following year, I had the opportunity to enter the Honors English class, an opportunity that would test my desire to take a chance and to put in the extra effort to succeed. Although my work in sophomore College Prep English had been vigorous and substantial, I doubted my ability to face the most challenging English class available. I consulted two teachers, and they both warned me that my grade would probably suffer in the honors class. Hearing the challenge in their words, I decided to take the risk in order to learn more, and I made the leap to the next level. After six weeks of devoted frustration, I received a C minus. My parents were worried that I was exceedingly burdened, but I was content with the level of competition and with the information and skills I was learning. In spite of—or perhaps because of—that initial grade, I wanted to show that I could not only survive, but succeed.

On the day of our last in-class essay, the speed with which my pen covered my originally blank piece of paper flashes in my mind like another mental photograph. I finished my essay in the time given. After countless nights of little sleep, I had caught up with the class, and I finally prevailed with an A minus. More importantly, I proved that challenging myself had been the right decision.

My struggle to succeed in high school was like trying to climb a very tall mountain, and my steep and difficult climb has brought me a great sense of accomplishment. Each minor accomplishment was like surmounting a smaller peak; one of those more frightening peaks to conquer was a 10-minute solo presentation on civil rights for Honors English. Keenly aware of my accent on certain words, I was clearly not born for public speaking. As the girl speaking before me finished her last words, I could feel my heart crashing against my chest, and the temperature of my hands dropped to absolute zero. I stood in front of my class, and 70 staring eyes pinned me as I tried to utter my first word. As I continued to speak, however, my frustration and discomfort abated. When I heard applause and saw smiles on my classmates' supportive faces, I was overwhelmed by pride and satisfaction. The intense effort had been worth the reward.

This triumphant image stays with me as I flip my photo album closed. "If you want to survive, you have to put in twice as much effort as anybody else." While I find that my father's words still echo truth, I have also found that with effort I can not only survive, but thrive. During this seemingly short period of time studying in Burlingame High School, I have found the confidence and the strength to take on any challenge that life may offer me.

Why This Essay Succeeded

Nenhan's essay really takes you inside his head to share his thoughts, fears and emotions as he faced each new trial. He helps you understand how he could become motivated enough to raise his grade from a C to an A. This is also a very good decision since the admission officers might wonder about his low grades early on in high school. But after reading his essay they would not only understand his transcript better but would be even more impressed at his turnaround. Nenhan's essay fulfills two goals: it provides context for his achievements and shows his ability to overcome challenges. Both are highly desirable by colleges looking for good students.

Kelly Y. Tanabe

Cerritos, California

When writing her essay, Kelly, the co-author of this book, remembered the painful experience she had in elementary school when she made her first presentation to the class. With moist palms and butterflies in her stomach, she anxiously read the words on the index cards. Kelly vowed that she would become a writer so that she could express herself fully through words on paper if not always aloud. At Whitney High School, she became the editor of the newspaper, assistant editor of the yearbook and worked with the local library to start a reading program for elementary school children. And she made many more presentations to the class, growing more comfortable each time.

My Voice
Harvard University

I have a soft voice. When I was younger, I did not like to present oral reports to my class because my voice did not carry. I have always desired a powerful voice, a voice that beckoned others to listen, captivated them and provoked them into absorbing the thoughts I expressed.

I was not born with this voice.

For this reason, I have turned to writing. For me, my voice is projected through the words I write. Since I wrote my first article for my elementary school newspaper at the age of 8, I have had a passion for journalism.

Through my school newspaper, *Aspects*, I grew acquainted with the field of journalism. As the Editor of this self-funded work, I learned the steps necessary to produce a publication—from the conception of articles to the distribution of the paper.

This background with *Aspects* developed in me the desire to continue my growth as a journalist. For this reason, I plan to develop my communications abilities in college as well as to write for a publication upon my graduation. With this education at Harvard and Radcliffe, I hope that my writing skills will progress in order to prepare for my future in the field.

With this education, I hope to hone my voice. I want others to listen, to hear my ideas, to have their lives affected by the articles that I write. For while the words that I speak are heard only once, the words that I write will be heard many times. Now, I have a powerful voice.

Why This Essay Succeeded

Since this is my (Kelly's) essay I can add some thoughts on how I wrote it and what I was trying to accomplish. My biggest challenge was the limited space. It's a problem that every student faces. I knew that I could only get in a few key points and I definitely wanted one of them to be my work with the school newspaper. But I also knew that this could be problematic since there were literally thousands of high school journalists applying to college. So how could I make my essay unique?

The answer came when I did some self-reflection into why I enjoyed writing and how I felt when I wrote. When I thought about it I realized that I loved writing because it gave my voice—which was soft—volume. I could be heard through my writing in ways that I never could be in person. So that became my introduction and how I would make my essay unique.

Doing so also allowed me to work in the fact that I had been writing for a very long time. On the Harvard application I listed my involvement in the high school newspaper but there was no place to mention my writing before then. So my essay allowed me to include my earliest journalistic assignment at age 8. I hoped that this would show the admission officers that writing was something that was an integral part of the majority of my life.

Finally, I wanted to conclude the essay on a high note and show that my future was only just beginning. I wanted the admission officers to understand that as a college student I would continue to raise my voice through my writing (which I ultimately did working on the Harvard newspaper) and make myself heard.

Essays About Places

Emanuel Pleitez
El Sereno, California
In his essay, Emanuel appreciates the view from the top of a hill, where he goes to exercise and think. He has had a lot to balance in his life. At Woodrow Wilson High School, he was the captain of five varsity athletic teams and earned 19 varsity letters. A first-generation college student, he was raised by his single mother, an immigrant from Mexico. His efforts have resulted in him not only getting into his dream college but also winning almost $30,000 in merit-based scholarships. Emanuel hopes to enter politics or return to teach at his high school.

My Hill
Stanford University

I am pumping my arms, trying to keep my legs moving. I feel lightheaded and frail needing to catch my breath, but I am only half the way up. I will not stop. I will keep going and going until I reach the top. These are some of the feelings I get as I am running up my hill. The community of El Sereno, which I live in, is full of hills. The biggest one with the antennae on top is "my hill." I use it to work out, to reflect upon things and just to be alone. As I am running up my hill, I remember how hard my mom has worked all her life for my sister and me. I remember playing basketball as a fifth grader amongst teenagers and grown men, learning to believe in myself and to stay on the right path. When I reach the top I look around and appreciate the beauty, tradition and all the hard workers of my community. I realize that I am part of it. I must contribute to the tradition and give back.

Sometimes I feel that I am not in tip-top shape, but I know I must be to play all my sports. At these times I say to myself, "Let's hit the hill." I have to work the hardest. That is just how I am. This comes from my mom. I always think of her when I am running my hill. She is the hardest worker I know. I remember the times we got off the bus at 10 o'clock at night coming from downtown L.A. after a full day of shopping for the things my mom sold throughout the week to support us. We would still have to walk about a mile as my mom carried my little sister and a bag in one arm and held me by the other hand while I carried another bag. Besides earning a living, my mom went to school to learn English. She has gone to school for as long as my sister and I to try to earn her high school diploma. Even though it has been a tough road, she has never given up. I take that feeling with me going up my hill and in life.

Another reflection I have when I am on my hill is of when I was a fifth grader playing basketball every day at my elementary school until it was too dark to see anything. All the older guys would come and play too. They tossed me around, but it made me tough. I will not be afraid of anything after playing with them. It was a great challenge, and I love challenges. They taught me to believe in myself and never let anything put me down. They were not the greatest of role models as they did drugs and basically did not have a future, but they always talked to me as if I was their little boy. I could have ended up like them as other childhood friends have, but I just took the advice and stayed on the right path. One guy told me, "Keep on practicing and one day you can make it to the NBA." I probably will not be a professional basketball player, but just the belief that they had and actually still have in me has given me the boost to always excel. Being on my hill helps me reflect upon what has shaped me in my community.

On top of my hill I can see all of El Sereno on one side and the rest of Los Angeles on the other. I love to look at my community, especially my high school. My high school represents the place in which I live. It represents the whole community, as it holds our future. It also holds our past, as many of our teachers are Wilson alumni. It is a great tradition at our school that allows our teachers to teach with more passion since they are back to where they started. They really want to help our youth and that is what makes the place where I live special. It has shaped me to look at life as a mission to help people succeed. It has given me a positive outlook that has motivated me to give back to my community as much as I can as I get older.

My hill gives me my motivation, lets me reflect on my past and lets me see the future. It is a long journey in life as it is a long run up the hill. My hill starts off pretty easy, although I cannot see how far it is or where exactly I am headed because of the tall grass. Eventually though, I see the top and what path I have to take to get there, but I realize I still have a long way to go. I face obstacles and doubts, but I do not let them stop me. I am determined. When I get to the top, always knowing that I will, I feel unstoppable. I know the hard work will pay off.

Why This Essay Succeeded

A location can be a powerful topic for an essay because you can make connections between all of the sights, sounds and even smells and your life. Emanuel creates a touching portrait of his family and himself through the vignette of the views he sees from the top of the hill. By using the hill as an analogy, he is able to show the admission officers a number of different vistas of his life that otherwise would not ordinarily be related. Through each of the views—his family's late-night shopping trips, playing basketball and his high school—Emanuel is able to share what is really important to him and what he has gained from each experience. And that's really all that the admission officers are asking for in an essay.

Gabriel D. Carroll

The Crossroads
University of Chicago

Down around the intersection of Broadway and Embarcadero, between the chimneys and the channel, lies one of the few scenes that Oakland displays with pride to the outside world. It is Jack London Square, a 10-block area occupied by shops and offices, which looks out on the Alameda Channel and, beyond it in an appropriate direction, on San Francisco Bay. It is the site of numerous happenings, from the weekly Farmers' Market to the Fourth of July fireworks, and for the remaining time it somehow maintains an air of hospitality—even festivity—foreign to most of the city. But to me, the Square is more than a physical location; it has a variety of connotations, all somehow connected to Oakland.

It is not accurate to say that Jack London Square is a symbol of Oakland; rather, it is a gathering place for a variety of individual representatives of the intellectual and economic mediocrity on which the city frugally survives. To one side is the Port of Oakland, the heart of the city's commercial significance. It irritates me that this metropolis of 400,000 functions as a distribution center, a mere intermediary for the business of the outside world. The largest store on the Square is the Barnes & Noble, but I prefer to frequent its smaller counterpart in downtown Berkeley; the selection at the

Oakland site I find generally too mainstream and not particularly enlightened. Several years ago, when the Cirque du Soleil presented their performance, "Quidam," in Oakland, they were honored with a colossal statue in the Square of the show's protagonist, a headless man. I found headlessness particularly appropriate in a city whose public school system is justifiably lambasted in the headlines at regular intervals. If you go north on Broadway, you pass several adult-video stores. There is a homeless man here, a huge man smothered in blankets, sitting impassively near the entrance to the underground parking lot. This is what Jack London Square is: a point of convergence for things that, for better or for worse, are Oakland.

The irony is that, despite the implications of these symbols, I like Oakland. It is home. It offers me a sense of familiarity, of being somewhere. It contributes to my sense of identity. In the summer, when I come home from warmer places, it is refreshing to inhale the brisk air and know that I am in Oakland. Moreover, I have a tendency to assume the vantage point of the observer as often as that of the participant; I thus can look at Oakland's eccentricities in amusement. Why is it that East Oakland covers approximately half the city's area (and its position relative to the remaining portion is more southerly than easterly), while West Oakland is a tiny corner? Why is "East" Oakland full of numbered avenues running east to west, while, in the northern part of the city, east to west are numbered streets, and the numbers increase in the opposite direction? Caring to contemplate such trivia is what makes me identify with the city. And as for the pessimism I appear to glean from Jack London Square—well, this place is not that bad. Perhaps I say this only because familiarity induces one to come up with defenses, but Oakland tries. It takes pride in the commercial vitality that does exist. It enjoys its ethnocultural diversity despite being plagued by racial contention. The name of the Square—for indeed Jack London did spend part of his life here—reminds one that, historically, Oakland has been somehow important. Finding positive sides to the city adds to that inexplicable sense of satisfied familiarity.

Jack London Square suggests the whole city to me in another, more personal way. I have a habit of taking "urban hikes." Walking around provides physical exercise. It also is essential to cognition—I use long walks to work on math problems, musical compositions, planned additions to my website, school essays or just to introspect aimlessly on the events of the past few days. I find fresh air much more conducive to these activities than the cramped indoors. And it allows me to take in the sights and sounds of the city. One of my favorite destinations is Jack London Square, not because of the terminus itself so much as the process of getting there. From my house, the walk is an hour each way, and it traverses Oakland. I walk by Lake Merritt, the county courthouse, the public library, the museum, the BART subway station and a dim building whose barely discernible plaque reads "City of Oakland Electric Department, 1911"; across Chinatown, under Highway 880, past huge, barren-walled warehouses and by the Amtrak station. Though any feeling of having absolutely seen the entire city is illusory, experiencing these different facets still justifies and augments the sense of familiarity, and Jack London Square provides an excuse to do so.

Am I permanently tied to Oakland? No. When I am away from home, I can hardly claim a longing to return. In fact, I feel a fresh desire to explore, to know the ins and outs of my new environment and to find the same sort of indicators of the social and cultural entity that constitutes whatever other city as I have done in Oakland. What I experience is perhaps nothing more than a form of academic interest. Just as I have tried to expand my academic experience—while focusing on mathematics, I have also taken interest in chess, CX debate and programming, among other things—I want to know other places as well. I am not an inseverable part of Oakland. But it is a part of me, a fragment of my experience and my identity. Years from now, after I have finished college and graduate school, perhaps long after that, it is quite likely that I will return to Oakland. I will make the pilgrimage on foot to Jack London Square. And I will sit at one of the outdoor tables of the Barnes & Noble Café, sipping an Italian soda and remember what Oakland is.

Why This Essay Succeeded

From his essay, the admission officers can tell that Gabriel is extremely observant. He finds meaningful insights in his surroundings that others often overlook. In addition, he is able to recognize both the positive and negative aspects of his community, and yet he embraces them all. He is not judgmental but instead accepting–which is a valuable asset. Given that Gabriel's primary talent is mathematics this essay is an excellent showcase of his writing skill–which is often lacking in typical science types. If you know that English is not your strong point or that people may stereotype you as a science nerd who can't write, you need to spend extra effort on perfecting your essay. Gabriel leaves no doubt in the admission officer's mind that he is talented in both science and writing. While this may not have been easy, it was certainly worth the extra effort.

CHAPTER EIGHT

PARTING WORDS

In this chapter you will learn:

- Why you can write a breathtaking essay

- How final admission decisions are made

You Can Write A Breathtaking Essay

After we finished writing our last two books, *Get Into Any College* and *Get Free Cash For College*, we thought long and hard about what our next book should be. We asked ourselves, "When we were applying to colleges, what was the most difficult part?" While we agreed that the interviews were nerve-wracking and filling out the application forms took more bottles of white-out than necessary, the biggest challenge was clearly the essay.

When we were writing our essays we agonized for weeks over what to write about and had many false starts. It was the first time that we had to reflect on the 17 years of our lives and capsulize a single memorable moment into one page of text. And it was the first time that an essay would play such an important role in shaping the rest of our lives.

It became pretty clear that this should be our next book.

In writing this book we met many wonderful students and admission officers who shared their experiences and essays. The students we interviewed have written at least six essays. Each admission officer that we spoke with has read thousands, if not tens of thousands, of essays in his or her career. There was certainly no shortage of expertise.

To take a big step back and look at the process from a distance, we see that there is no single, correct way to write a successful essay. This is because the best essays are a reflection of their writers. Just as no two people are the same, no two great essays are the same either.

There are similar qualities (i.e., originality, passion, reflection, good writing) common to all successful essays, of course, and we have done our best to highlight these throughout the book. But when it comes time for you to write your essay, it will be an original. In some respects it will share the qualities of all of the essays featured in this book, but in many ways it will be totally different.

While we believe that sharing the 57 successful essays in this book is a vital part of learning what makes a great essay, we want to underscore the fact that these are not the only ways to write a great essay. Incorporate the lessons that you learn from these essays. Study the

How Final Decisions Are Made

The former senior associate director of admissions at Yale University reveals what it all comes down to when deciding whom to admit

We want to share some insights from Lloyd Peterson, former senior associate director of admissions at Yale, former dean of admissions at Vassar College and director of education at College Coach.

We asked Peterson what the decision comes down to once admission officers have everything about the applicant, including their essay, laid out in front of them. He says, "In the end we often have to ask very nuanced questions about each applicant. There are three major categories that we ask about.

"First, is this a good institution-to-student fit? Is your value system in line with that of my institution? Colleges and universities can be like teenagers. They all have their own personalities, and we want to make sure that a student would thrive in the environment of our school.

"Second, can the student do the work? This is pretty obvious, and many students meet this requirement—but then again some will do better than others.

"Finally, can our school meet the student's needs outside of the classroom? We want to make sure that you will be happy."

But where do you find these answers? Peterson admits, "Most of these answers do not come from transcripts and SATs."

This has some important implications. If you are a student with high grades and test scores, you can't rely on these alone to get you into college. If you have less-than-perfect scores and grades, don't give up without even trying.

No matter which type of student you are, use your essay and the rest of your application to make a strong case for yourself and convince admission officers like Peterson that you deserve to be at their school.

strategies and mistakes that we present in each chapter. Contemplate the advice from the admission officers. Then go out and write your own masterpiece.

We leave you with one final observation. From our own experience writing admission essays and from that of the many students we interviewed, the one thing we never found was a student who after thinking long and hard said, "I don't have anything good to write about." No matter where you grew up or what you experienced, you have the raw material to create a unique and powerful essay. But you do need to think.

Admission officers and students who have written great essays stress over and over that to write a good essay you need to think. You can't just sit in front of the computer and expect a great essay to pour from your fingertips. You need to allow time for ideas to percolate and develop.

It was not uncommon among the students we interviewed for them to have revised their essays more than a dozen times over the course of several months. Between each revision they would think about what they had written and push themselves to analyze more. For many, including ourselves, the writing of the college admission essay took us to places and made us realize things about ourselves that we never knew existed when we first sat down to write.

This is as it should be. This is what the admission officers hope you accomplish. Relish the challenge. Savor the chance to share a part of yourself on paper. Remember, the admission officers really want to let you into their college. Give them a reason. Let your essay help open the doors.

APPENDIX: WEB RESOURCES

SuperCollege.com
www.supercollege.com
The publisher of this book. On SuperCollege.com you can get more help on getting into and paying for college. Plus, you can search a free database of thousands of scholarships and enter to enter the SuperCollege student scholarship.

OWL–Online Writing Lab
http://owl.english.purdue.edu
Articles and tips on writing from Purdue University. Also includes downloadable presentations on a variety of writing topics.

Guide to Grammar and Style
http://andromeda.rutgers.edu/
~jlynch/Writing/
An excellent reference that will answer all your tough grammar- and style-related questions.

Online Thesaurus
www.thesaurus.com
Find the perfect word by search-ing the online resource.

Merriam-Webster Online
www.webster.com
Allows you to look up words in a collegiate dictionary and thesau-rus.

Elements of Style
http://www.bartleby.com/141/
This is a classic reference text on usage and style. At some point you'll actually want to get the book since you'll be using it throughout college.

Columbia World of Quotations
http://education.yahoo.com/
reference/quotations/
If you are looking for a quote, try this Yahoo! index.

College Board
www.collegeboard.com
The makers of the SAT and PSAT offer articles on selecting colleges, completing your applications and test-taking.

Common Application
www.commonapp.org
See which schools accept the Common Application and download the necessary forms.

CollegeAnswer.com
www.collegeanswer.com
Provides information on selecting colleges, test prep and applying. Also provides a free scholarship database and financial aid calculators.

INDEX

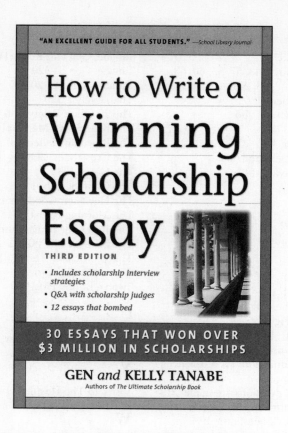

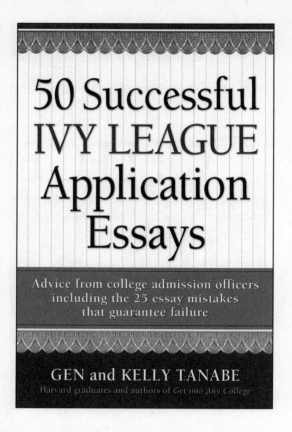

Attention Students:
Win The SuperCollege.com Scholarship

Each year SuperCollege awards scholarships to high school and college undergraduates who excel in both academics and extracurricular activities. These scholarships are a part of the ongoing mission of SuperCollege to help students get into and pay for the college of their dreams. To apply, visit **www.supercollege.com**. Good luck!

To get more secrets, tips and strategies on getting into and paying for college please visit **www.supercollege.com**. Just look at what you'll find:

- Apply for the SuperCollege.com Scholarship.
- Search for scholarships that match your background in a free database of thousands of awards.
- Learn more tips and strategies on college admission, financial aid and scholarships.
- Parents: Get advice on how you can help your child get into and pay for any college.
- Ask Gen and Kelly Tanabe your most pressing questions.

Visit us at www.supercollege.com for free resources on college admission, scholarships and financial aid.

About The Authors

Harvard graduates Gen and Kelly Tanabe are the founders of SuperCollege and the award-winning authors of 13 books including: *The Ultimate Scholarship Book, Get Into Any College, The Ultimate Guide to America's Best Colleges, Get Free Cash for College* and *50 Successful Ivy League Application Essays.*

Together, Gen and Kelly were accepted to every school to which they applied, including all of the Ivy League colleges, and won over $100,000 in merit-based scholarships. They were able to leave Harvard debt-free and their parents guilt-free.

Gen and Kelly give workshops at high schools across the country and write the nationally syndicated "Ask The SuperCollege.com Experts" column. They have made dozens of appearances on television and radio and have served as expert sources for respected publications including *U.S. News & World Report, USA Today, The New York Times, Chicago Sun-Times, New York Daily News, Chronicle of Higher Education* and *Seventeen.*

Gen grew up in Waialua, Hawaii. Between eating banana-flavored shave ice and basking in the sun, he was president of the Student Council, captain of the Speech Team and a member of the tennis team. A graduate of Waialua High School, he was the first student from his school to be accepted at Harvard. In college, Gen was chair of the Eliot House Committee and graduated *magna cum laude* with a degree in both History and East Asian Studies.

Kelly attended Whitney High School, a nationally ranked public high school in her hometown of Cerritos, California. She was the editor of the school newspaper, assistant editor of the yearbook and founder of a public service club to promote literacy. In college, she was the co-director of the HAND public service program and the brave co-leader of a Brownie Troop. She graduated *magna cum laude* with a degree in Sociology.

Gen, Kelly, their sons Zane and Kane and their dog Sushi live in Belmont, California.